"I am grateful for every minute I spent in the delightful company of Diana Joseph. I picked up her memoir late one afternoon, and proceeded to ignore my children, my dinner, and even my bedtime. I gobbled it up in a single sitting. Funny and poignant, it's a real treat."

—Ayelet Waldman, author of *Bad Mother*

"Despite the mouthful of a title, there isn't an excess word in this smart and tightly constructed debut. Fans of David Sedaris and Sarah Vowell will appreciate Joseph's portraits of the men in her life. From her young son's trench foot to her blue-collar father's attempt at a sex talk, these impeccably detailed stories are as heartfelt as they are trenchantly funny."

—*Library Journal* (starred review)

"Joseph adeptly scrutinizes the often opposing female and male sensibilities. She has a great eye for telling details that complete a character or scene."

—*Publishers Weekly*

"Diana Joseph's book is gritty, elegiac, and witty—a paean to the many ways in which we all love and ache. . . . Her keenly observant writing is compassionate yet utterly without sentimentality. *I'm Sorry You Feel That Way* begins slowly and simply, then builds like a symphony. Its uncommon, everyday love stories are peopled with flawed, compelling characters who reflect the author's own humanity like shards of mirror, creating a work of unexpected power and truth."

—Susan Jane Gilman,
author of *Undress Me in the Temple of Heaven*
and *Hypocrite in a Pouffy White Dress*

"She never lionizes suffering. Instead, she sifts through the ruins of her romantic and emotional entanglements, with an eye on the absurdities we endure in the name of love."

—*Los Angeles Times*

I'm Sorry
You Feel That Way

The Astonishing but True Story of a
Daughter, Sister, Slut, Wife, Mother,
and Friend to Man and Dog

Diana Joseph

Berkley Books, New York

THE BERKLEY PUBLISHING GROUP
Published by the Penguin Group
Penguin Group (USA) Inc.
375 Hudson Street, New York, New York 10014, USA
Penguin Group (Canada), 90 Eglinton Avenue East, Suite 700, Toronto, Ontario M4P 2Y3, Canada
(a division of Pearson Penguin Canada Inc.)
Penguin Books Ltd., 80 Strand, London WC2R 0RL, England
Penguin Group Ireland, 25 St. Stephen's Green, Dublin 2, Ireland (a division of Penguin Books Ltd.)
Penguin Group (Australia), 250 Camberwell Road, Camberwell, Victoria 3124, Australia
(a division of Pearson Australia Group Pty. Ltd.)
Penguin Books India Pvt. Ltd., 11 Community Centre, Panchsheel Park, New Delhi—110 017, India
Penguin Group (NZ), 67 Apollo Drive, Rosedale, North Shore 0632, New Zealand
(a division of Pearson New Zealand Ltd.)
Penguin Books (South Africa) (Pty.) Ltd., 24 Sturdee Avenue, Rosebank, Johannesburg 2196,
South Africa

Penguin Books Ltd., Registered Offices: 80 Strand, London WC2R 0RL, England

Some names and identifying characteristics have been changed. Some sequences and details of events have been changed. The publisher does not have any control over and does not assume any responsibility for author or third-party websites or their content.

Grateful acknowledgment is made to the following, where portions of this book first appeared: *Willow Springs*: "The Devil I Know Is the Man Upstairs"; *River Teeth*: "It's Me. It's Him. It's Them."; *Weber*: "What's (Not) Simple"; *Marginalia*: "The Boy."

PRINTING HISTORY
Amy Einhorn/G. P. Putnam's Sons hardcover edition / March 2009
Berkley trade paperback edition / February 2010

Berkley trade paperback ISBN: 978-0-425-23221-7

The Library of Congress has cataloged the hardcover edition as follows:

Joseph, Diana, date.
I'm sorry you feel that way : the astonishing but true story of a daughter, sister, slut, wife, mother, and friend to man and dog / Diana Joseph.
p. cm.
ISBN 978-0-399-15528-4
1. Joseph, Diana, date. 2. Joseph, Diana, date—Philosophy. 3. Joseph, Diana, date—Family. 4. Authors, American—21st century—Biography. 5. Women—United States—Biography. 6. Feminists—United States—Biography. 7. Joseph, Diana, date—Marriage. 8. Man-woman relationships—United States. 9. Motherhood—United States. I. Title.
PS3610.O668Z46 2009 2008026146
814'.6—dc22

PRINTED IN THE UNITED STATES OF AMERICA

10 9 8 7 6 5 4 3 2 1

*Penguin is committed to publishing works of quality and integrity.
In that spirit, we are proud to offer this book to our readers;
however, the story, the experiences, and the words
are the author's alone.*

For The Boy
and For Allen

Contents

A man is a god in ruins.

—RALPH WALDO EMERSON

I'm Sorry You Feel That Way

Tongue Twister,
Tongue Tied

One day my father sat me down and said, "See, what happens is sometimes a girl will go with this one, and then she'll go with that one, and then she thinks what the hell, that one over there doesn't look so bad, why not go with that one, too."

My father paused to take a long draw on his cigarette. It was 1982, the "Just Say No" campaign hadn't yet come on full-force, and fathers like mine smoked without guilt or shame or brainwashed children nagging at them to quit. They smoked in front of their children and their children's friends, they smoked in the station wagon with children bouncing around in the backseat, the baby sitting on somebody's lap and all the windows rolled up. A sixth-grader could walk to the corner convenience store to play the Daily Number and buy a pack of smokes; no one questioned it. My father played 0-2-6, a dollar straight and a dollar boxed. He smoked Lucky Strikes, unfiltered. I walked the eight blocks from my house to the Fast and Friendly to play his number and buy his Luckies just about every day.

My father was talking, he was explaining something. There was something important that I needed to know, and he was telling me about it. I needed to listen. He wanted me to pay attention.

"Now, look," my father said, "when a girl goes with this one, and then with that one, and then with that one over there, and with who knows how many others, what happens is people start to talk. People will always hear all about what she did, see, and when they do, they'll talk about it. They'll say that girl is a pig."

The Lucky dangled from my father's lips and his eyes were squinty from the smoke. He raised his eyebrows. He was jabbing his finger at me. Moving only half his mouth, my father said, "Don't be a pig."

That was the first time my father ever talked to me about sex. It would be his final word on the matter. Neither he nor I would speak of it again.

M y father has spoken to me about other things. He is a man of firm belief and definite opinion.

For a long time, one of his favorite issues to put on the table was the ratio of how little money I make to how much education I have. He liked to ask how much was I making, so he could say, "That's it?" and then taunt me. "I'm the dummy," he'd say, "and I made more than that. You're supposed to have all this education. What was all that schooling for if that's all the money you're going to make?"

My father, who dropped out of school in eighth grade, owned

and operated a tow truck and auto body shop. When I was a kid, he loomed large, big and tall, powerful and strong, his energy endless, but these days, his health isn't good. He's given his retirement over to puttering around the house, he's cooking fabulous meals, baking fabulous pies—even rolling out his own crust—and he dabbles with day trading online.

Usually, when I call home, my mother answers the phone. She's the one I chat with, the one I ask how's Dad doing? or what's Dad been up to? If it's Father's Day or his birthday, I call specifically to speak to him, and usually I can get him on the phone to wish him Merry Christmas.

But there have been times, though rare, when I've called home, and my mother isn't there. My father answers the phone. That's when he and I talk.

This happens once, maybe twice, a year. During these conversations, my father has spoken with great authority and discussed at great length matters I can't begin to comprehend: investments and annuities, bonds and interest rates, the Fed, the Dow Jones, and the stock market, which I always hear as the *stalk* market. I imagine a small creepy one-room office across the river and in the questionable part of town. It's where I'd go if I wanted to hire someone to keep menacingly close tabs on someone else. I'm running through the many possibilities of who I'd like to have stalked when I hear my father say how much money do you have in your savings?

The honest answer would be none, I don't have any money in my savings. I don't have a savings account, and if you really want to know, the way I balance my checkbook is by changing banks.

But I'm a coward. My answers to the questions my father asks are rarely honest. Because I'm all about keeping the old man off my back, I'm all about telling him what I think he wants to hear. I also want him to think well of me, which means the truth will not do.

"Eighteen hundred," I say every time he asks, because it sounds like a figure that's plausible and realistic, like it could be true, but it also sounds, to me at least, like an impressive amount of money to have just lying around. "Almost two thousand dollars saved!" I tell my father, who, in turn, always says the same thing. He always says, "Not enough."

During these telephone conversations, my father and I also talk about my brothers. My father confides in me his feelings concerning my brothers' lives, specifically what they're doing wrong.

"He's an asshole," my father says.

I don't have to ask which brother he's talking about. I know that if I'm patient, at some point, my father will reveal to me that both of my brothers are assholes, but each boy is an asshole in his own special way. I never disagree with my father on this matter. I never take up for my brothers, I don't defend them or argue their cases. I always defer to my father's opinion, murmuring my agreement that my brother is an asshole indeed, no bones about it. I mean my brothers no harm, but I'm happier when my father is displeased with someone other than me.

While I have wandered from Pennsylvania to New York to Colorado to Minnesota, both of my brothers still live near my parents. This makes it easy for my father to keep up with their lives. This is what enables him to point out with such certainty that my one brother is an asshole because his bitch of a girlfriend is leading him around by the balls, while my other brother is an asshole because of the truck he bought, or because of how fast he rides his motorcycle, or because he says it's fun to go four-wheeling. One of my brothers is an asshole because of the way he went about digging a hole, or hanging drywall, or building a deer stand, and my other brother is an asshole because he got pulled over for speeding, or because he thinks he's in love with a single mother seven years his senior.

"I tried to tell him," my father says, "but he's a hardhead. He thinks he knows everything. He doesn't know jack shit. But he won't listen to me. If he'd listen to me, he'd know."

"I know," I say. "It's true."

"He's an asshole."

"It's true."

My father says he doesn't need me to tell him what's true.

I agree.

If it's a rare thing for me to call home and talk to my father, it's even rarer when my father calls me. Each time it happens, it catches me off guard, and every time, I'm a little flattered, thinking wow, he must really want to talk to me. He must've been thinking about me. I'm charmed by it. I think it's cute that my father has taken the time to search for my phone number, then dial it. I think it's sweet. It makes me feel singled out, special, privileged, honored, and loved.

One time my father called to reveal that my mother didn't like being a stay-at-home mom, she didn't like being stuck at home with children. "Your mother doesn't like kids," he shared. "She never has."

Another time he called to say he hadn't been feeling well. "I feel funny lately," he told me. "I can't think, I can't sleep, I can't concentrate." His health problems require him to take a variety of prescription drugs. There are the pills he takes in the morning, the pills he takes at night; there are the pills he takes for pain, the pills he takes on an empty stomach or with food. Green pills, red pills, blue pills. "I just want you to know," my father continued, "I think it's her. She's doing something to my medicine. If I turn up dead," my father told me, "it's your mother."

I said thanks, Dad, I appreciate you letting me know, and thanks for calling, and after we hung up, I called my brother Mitchell. "I just got off the phone with Dad," I said. There was something smug in my tone. Something gleeful and gloating and proud. "Dad called me. He told me if he turns up dead, it's Mom."

But Mitchell already knew. Of course he'd already heard. "Dad called me this morning," he said, and I was immediately jealous and resentful. If I'm second to that asshole on the old man's list of allies, how special can I be?

T here are things about my father that I just don't know.
For example, I don't know how tall he is. I don't know how old he is. I don't know what my father wanted to be when he grew up, or who was his best friend when he was twelve.

I don't know who taught him to ride a bike. I don't know his favorite color. I don't know if he ever saw a rock concert or who his favorite Beatle was, or what he would have majored in if he'd gone to college. Business would be my guess, but is that right? Do I have it right?

I don't know how long he and my mother have been married, or when is their anniversary, or how they met, or the story of their courtship. I don't know his first wife's name or how it works that one of the four daughters from his first marriage is younger than me. I don't know how old he was when his father died or how he felt about the man.

I don't know how he'll feel about the words on this page.

I don't know how to find these things out unless I ask, and I don't know how to ask. I don't know what words I would say. I don't know where I would begin, and what if it turns out there are things I don't really want to know?

It's possible there are things I don't really want to know.

When I'm on the phone with my father, I listen. I say yes, yes. Right, right. Of course. It's true. How about that. Wow, I never thought of it like that. I agree with everything he says. These conversations last until my mother returns from wherever she's been—the store, usually—and my father says your mother's here, let me put your mother on the phone.

M y father is maybe six feet tall and he might be fifty-nine years old. He smokes. He has a two-pack-a-day habit, though he's tried to quit, more than once. During those times, his temper, while never mild, never gentle, was even shorter, more volatile. Just the words *Dad's quit* made us speak softly and step lightly. But the time he tried to light that artificial cigarette, the fake one made of plastic and meant to appeal to the smoker's oral fixation, he seemed embarrassed and maybe even a little amused.

My father likes food: pistachios and peanuts, sausage sandwiches and meatball sandwiches, ham sandwiches and Easter ham dotted with cloves and pineapple rings. He makes his spaghetti sauce from scratch; his chicken noodle soup stops the sniffles, cures cancer, and clears up acne. There are bottles and bottles of booze in our china cupboard, but my father doesn't drink. One time, I saw him have a beer with his dinner in a restaurant, but I have never seen him drunk. Instead, he drinks iced tea, all day long, all year round, sweet tea, made on the stove top: a saucepan of boiling water, a cup of sugar, ten Lipton tea bags.

My father's eyes are blue. His legs are skinny. His hair is curly and black, though he's balding, and has been for as long as I can remember, a bald spot on the back of his head that we measured first with a quarter, then a silver dollar, then the rim of a cup, and now it's just a big bald spot.

When I was little, I used to give him a pack of Lucky Strikes for Christmas, or a lottery ticket, a wallet, socks, or a package of T-shirts. The T-shirts had to have a pocket for his cigarettes. I rarely saw him wear any other kind of shirt. I have never seen him in a suit.

Around the house, he doesn't wear a shirt. Every night, as soon as my father came home from work, he took off his shirt. His stomach was large and round and hairy, fat but hard. He had the kind of gut that allowed him to say Punch me. Go ahead. As hard as you want, as hard as you can. I was so used to seeing him like this that I didn't think anything of it, not until years later when I was an adult, and a friend, flipping through my family album, pointed out there isn't hardly a picture of my old man where he's wearing a shirt. Not in Christmas pictures or the pictures from his birthday party, and not in the picture I have of us on my graduation day, me in my cap and gown, and my father, shirtless.

He didn't bother to put on a shirt when a boy came to pick me up for a date. The rule was a boy couldn't just sit out in the driveway and wait for me, he had to come in the house and say hello to my father, shirtless and big-bellied, my father who didn't necessarily acknowledge my date, didn't always put the newspaper down, sometimes didn't turn down the volume on the television or even turn his head in the boy's direction. Once, after seeing the bologna-skin tires on one boy's car, my father refused to allow me to go anywhere until that kid got a new set. Another boy asked me if my father was mean. Sometimes, I said. Still another asked if my father hated him. I said I didn't know. It seemed possible, especially since I wasn't always sure how my father felt about me.

My father worked long, hard hours. My brothers and I grew up to be people who don't quite know what to do with ourselves when we're not working. When my father came home from work, he wanted his children to greet him at the door. He wanted a sheet spread across the couch so the couch stayed clean while he took a nap before supper. He wanted a supper that included meat, starch, vegetable, and a stack of sliced white bread on a saucer, a stick of soft oleo in the butter dish. He wanted to watch television in peace.

My father watched Paul Kangas host *Nightly Business Report* on PBS. He watched movies about vigilantes and renegade cops, and he especially liked Chuck Norris movies or movies starring Charles Bronson or anything with Clint Eastwood as a cop or a cowboy. On Sunday afternoons, my father watched football games and he liked *Kung Fu*, the series where a monk named Kwai Chang Caine wandered through the American West, occasionally experiencing flashbacks in which he remembers some valuable lesson taught to him by blind Master Po. My father brought home a VHS tape called *Faces of Death* that showed a scene of people eating a monkey's brains fresh out of its skull. My brothers and I weren't allowed to watch it, but the old man told us about the people who, forks in hand, dug right in.

I also have the impression my father liked the film *Purple Rain*, starring Prince, which he must have caught one of the zillion times it ran on HBO.

Am I remembering right? Can that possibly be true?

As far as I know, my father doesn't read books for pleasure, but he's always read the newspaper. He likes to look at real estate listings from other parts of the country and compare prices to where he lives. When I travel I always pick one up for him, though I almost never get it mailed, and when I eventually toss it in the recycling bin, I feel guilty. I feel like I should try harder. I should do more.

When I was growing up, my father seemed unapproachable and unpredictable. Sometimes he got really, really furious about something—dust on top of the grandfather clock, for example, or that the pork chops my mother made for supper had been frozen, or the C that I got in algebra—and he'd yell. Or he would throw something. He might ridicule someone until that person cried. He might hit something. He might hit someone.

It's easy to remember the mean things my father did. The violent things, the hard, angry things. Growing up the daughter of such a man, it's easy to fixate on those things, to hold a grudge. Letting go of the grudge is much more difficult. One of my brothers tells me Dad's not like that anymore, the old man has really mellowed out. My other brother says he just wants everybody to be happy and get along.

Such assholes!

So when I think about my father, I try to keep in mind the other things I know about him, the things I know for sure.

There's this:

My father could be a clown. He liked tongue twisters, and hearing him mangle them always made me laugh. He could say *A big black bug bled black blood.* He was good at *She sells sea shells down by the seashore.* But *Seashell city* tripped him up. *Seashell city. Seashell city. Seashell city.*

She smells shitty!

There's this:

My father and I were watching a video called, I think, *Cops: Too Hot for TV.* There was a sting operation involving undercover police disguised as Arab sheiks busting a prostitution ring. When I said surely members of law enforcement have better things to do than hassle those poor women, my father said he disagreed. Those poor women are criminals, he said. So I said prostitution should be legal.

I don't know why I said that. I don't even know if I believe it. I was twenty-five years old, old enough to have and assert a controversial opinion, but I suspect there was nothing grand or lofty about what I was saying. I think I was just trying to shock my father, get a reaction out of the old man, who said he was disappointed in me, he thought he had raised me better than that. He looked sad. He said do you have no morals? What happened to your morals? I wanted to raise you better than that.

And there's this:

One year my father made me watch the Jerry Lewis Labor Day Telethon to benefit the Muscular Dystrophy Association. I was fascinated by every detail. I remember how in the final hours, his hair black as shoe polish, slick with pomade, dapper tuxedoed Jerry loosened his bow tie, tugged open his collar, and made a case for the kids, his kids, those poor sad tragic hopeless crippled kids. Jerry sang "You'll Never Walk Alone." *You'll never walk, period* flashed through my mind, and as if to punish my wicked thoughts, my father pledged my allowance to the handicapped children on my behalf. He asked if I understood how lucky I was that I could talk and walk and sit up straight. I imagined how awful it would be to be handicapped in a wheelchair or on crutches, and I felt happy that I wasn't. Then I felt guilty about my happiness, guilty about my good fortune, my healthy body, my strong mind. Then I felt resentful about how it wasn't my fault that I possessed good fortune, healthy body, strong mind, and who were Jerry's Kids to get my allowance? Then I felt ashamed of my selfishness. I broke open my piggy bank and threw some Susan B. Anthony silver dollars at the problem. I became a Democrat because of my father, who keeps how he votes to himself.

And finally, there's this:

My father is the smartest man I know. He remembers things he learned in fifth, sixth, seventh grade, things like how many feet are in a mile and how many cups are in a gallon and what's the state capital of North Dakota. He wanted me to know things, too: how to work out math problems in my head and why I should pay attention to interest rates, what my constitutional rights include and why I need to pay off my credit cards in full every month. He told me to trust no one, that the United States government wants me to be ignorant and stay ignorant, and that the media are trying to keep me that way, and so is corporate America, and so is the pope. He told me if I ever wanted to make some real money, I should major in business, not English. He believed college wasn't really even necessary, and he said if I went into business, then I needed to learn to play golf because the big business deals are made on the golf course. Shortly before I moved to Syracuse, New York, my father told me that someday the entire state of New York will be underwater. He told me gas prices will drop in the weeks before an election. He told me to always carry enough money to make a phone call or pay a cab for a ride home. He told me to always carry some form of ID in my pocket so they can identify my body if I'm ever in a disfiguring accident. He told me no one is more important than my family.

What happens is sometimes a girl will go with this one, and he isn't right for her, so she'll go with that one, and she doesn't like him, either. The girl isn't a pig, she just doesn't know what she wants. Or maybe she is a pig, but she's young and reckless and doesn't care. She likes romance, she wants adventure. She sees that one over there, and he doesn't look so bad. In fact, he looks to her like he's pretty good, and she thinks what the hell, why not.

So I went with that one. But my father didn't like him, didn't approve of him, and for a long time, my father didn't speak to me. Not even on Father's Day when I showed up with a wrapped gift box containing a leather wallet. Not even when I said Happy Father's Day, Dad. It took me getting knocked up before my father grudgingly spoke to me again.

I named my son for him. My son's middle name is my father's first name. I think my father appreciated the gesture, but then I don't know for sure. He's never said.

A friend of mine once told me to give it up, he was sick of hearing me go on about it. "Your old man is never going to love you the way you think he should," my friend said. "He's never going to ask the questions you want him to ask. The best thing you can do is learn to father yourself."

The father I've invented for myself is sitting at the kitchen table, shirtless and drinking iced tea. He's eating pistachios, his fingers are stained red. It's the summer of 1982. I'm twelve years old, and I'm hot and sweaty and just coming home from pretending my bike is really a palomino named Goldie. There's a pile of stubbed-out Luckies littering the ashtray, there's a Lucky hanging from his mouth. It's been a long day towing cars out of ditches and painting cars in a sunless, claustrophobic garage. His hands have been scrubbed with a brush and some Goop, his shoulders are stiff, the tendons in his neck are tight, he's got a headache, his back hurts, he looks tired.

Hi, Daddy, I say.

My father smiles. Hi, sweetheart, he says. He pats the seat beside him. He says what's new with you?

The Boy

Recently, the boy showed me his feet. They were disgusting. They oozed, but they also looked dry. He said his feet were itchy and that they hurt. It hurt to stand, he said. It hurt to walk. He said he needed crutches or, even better, a motorized wheelchair. His feet smelled horrible, bringing to mind that Pablo Neruda poem about the blood of the children and how it's like the blood of the children. No metaphor can begin to describe the atrocity, no comparison can come close. The same idea was applicable here: the boy's terribly smelly feet smelled like terribly smelly feet.

What happened to your feet? I said. How did they get to be like this?

The boy said he didn't know.

We showed his feet to our next-door neighbor, a Vietnam veteran, who in one glance made a diagnosis: "My God! That's trench foot! I haven't seen that since Vietnam!"

The boy was interrogated. He blinked under the harsh light,

but he didn't flinch. He only said his feet hurt, and he didn't know how or why.

I know why. Though this boy has a dresser full of clean socks, fresh socks, neatly folded socks, he one day decided he'd wear again the pair he'd already been wearing. He got out of the shower and put those dirty socks back on. That night, he wore them to bed. The next day, he wore them to school.

If you ask the boy why, why would you do such a thing, he'll shrug. He'll smile. He'll say he doesn't know.

The boy with trench foot is my son. He was born on April 20, 1992, a few days before the L.A. riots. His birthday is also Hitler's birthday and the day of the shootings at Columbine High School. Other upsetting events around April 20 include the end of the siege of the Branch Davidian complex outside Waco, Texas, and the bombing of the federal court building in Oklahoma City. This bothers the boy. He believes that so many bad things having history on or around his birthday doesn't bode well for him or his future. He thinks it reveals a flaw in character: his own, of course, but also mine.

You know this boy. He was the one at the first T-ball practice who cried because he didn't know how to run the bases. At T-ball games, he sat tucked away far in the outfield, pulling up the grass, watching dreamily as the ball rolled by. You made assumptions about him. Thin and nervous. Asthmatic child of a chain-smoking mother. The kind of kid who'd stay pale all summer long.

But he might have surprised you. Though the boy didn't much care for T-ball, he refused to quit, no matter how many times I recommended it, no matter how much I encouraged it, not even when I offered him five dollars and a Happy Meal. I didn't want to believe his commitment to the sport was because of determination or spunk. We're not that kind of people. The boy sucked at T-ball. He knew this. Everyone knew this. I figured he played because of the postgame snacks: the Popsicles, the Rice Krispy Treats, the Dixie cups of purple Kool-Aid.

You also saw me at the T-ball games. I sat alone in the bleachers, the mother separate from other mothers—the sick, weak, puny antelope cut off by the rest of the herd. Those other mothers? They didn't invite me to their after-game picnics. When the sign-up sheet for bringing in the postgame snacks went around, it passed by me. None of them asked if we were signing up for soccer, and would I like to join the carpool.

At the time, it occurred to me I was being snubbed, though I wasn't good at figuring out why. Every once in a while, I glanced up from the novel I was reading or the crossword I was puzzling or the menthol cigarette I was smoking to hear female voices shrieking at my child: "C'mon! You can do it! Run, run, run! Hustle, hustle, hustle!"

I watched my son stroll to first. He plopped his bottom on the base, possibly exhausted, but more likely bored. "Get up!" those other mothers shrieked. "Where's your fighting spirit? Where's your hustle?"

I watched them pound their fists in the air like they were banging on a door or joining Communists in solidarity. I marveled at their enthusiasm. It was nice they cared, but it was a T-ball game, for Christ's sake, played by five-year-olds. I'd light up another smoke and get up from the bleachers to go sit someplace quieter, like my car. I waited for the T-ball game to end so I could go home and wait for T-ball season to end.

What you don't know is when T-ball season ended, the boy was bellyaching again. What surprised me was why. He was sad it was over. He liked T-ball. He liked his name in white letters across the back of his shirt. He liked how the players lined up to slap hands with the other team. He liked how everyone was nice, saying way to go, good job, good game.

There are other moments from which you know him, this boy, my son. He was the boy in kindergarten who freaked out a little girl by insisting he was her husband, she was his wife, they were married, and they would never get a divorce. This same year Monica Lewinsky was news, and when the boy asked me how to spell "sex," I told him, never figuring he'd go to school the next day and write it all over his alphabet journal, sometimes in large letters, sometimes in small, and sometimes upside down. This same year the boy's father and I got a divorce, and the boy reverted to thumb-sucking and took up grinding his teeth.

You might remember him from first grade: he's the one who ate glue. He and I were so broke that year that when he found a ten-dollar bill in the street, I took it from him, thrilled I could put gas in the tank. This boy believed in Santa and the Tooth Fairy and the Easter Bunny long after all the other boys and most of the girls wised up. The summer between second and third grade, he was the boy you saw on the United flight, Denver to Pittsburgh, the Minor Traveling Alone to spend summer with his father, and when the boy boarded that flight, he didn't look back, breaking his mother's heart.

Think back to fourth grade. There was the boy on the playground the bigger boys knocked down. The game is called Push, and the object is to push this kid down, and every time he tries to stand back up, you push him down again.

Tell those guys you don't like that, I suggested. Or go tell the teacher. Or stay down. They'll get tired and go away eventually.

The boy wanted to know if he should hit anyone. He said that's what the Vietnam vet next door told him to do.

Absolutely not, I said. We are not people who use violence to resolve conflict.

The boy said I didn't understand.

Why are those guys even pushing you down? I asked, and the boy said they just were. But why, I asked, there must be a reason, it can't be arbitrary, and the boy said it was. Well, hang in there, I told him.

But the boy preferred a war vet's advice. The boy came to like the way his own hand can curl into a fist. How that fist can bloody a nose.

This boy, my son, is eleven years old. Standing four-foot-eight and weighing seventy-three pounds, he shows no natural athletic ability, no physical coordination, though he has other amazing talents: wiggling his ears, curling his tongue, raising just one eyebrow. Supersonic hearing enables him to eavesdrop on conversations taking place behind closed doors.

He's also a cruel mimic. "I'll be Mom," he says, and he puts his hands on his hips and bops his head. "I am absolutely bone weary!" he cries. He's made his voice squeaky and shrill and, for some reason, southern. It's not how I sound, though I recognize the furrowed brow and bunched-up lips. "I mean, what I wouldn't do for a hot bath, a soft bed, and a stiff…cocktail!"

The boy has no interest in, or sense of, fashion, though he dislikes when I refer to what he's wearing as an "outfit." He's aware of Eminem, but prefers to push Matchboxes in the sandbox or sit in his room building fantastical flying machines out of Legos. His morning breath will gag you, but he doesn't have B.O. His skin is unblemished. He has dimples and his father's high forehead. He wears glasses and longs for contacts, though I don't approve of giving contacts to a person who can't remember to flush the toilet. He's a good-looking boy who is going to be a good-looking man. He's aware of it. He's not above using it, especially on the nuns at Holy Trinity Catholic School who let him turn in his homework late and the female bakers at City Market who give him extra cookies. His eyelashes are so long they bend against the lenses in his glasses. His lips are pouty and red. He can look mournful, desolate, despairing, and in need of comfort, though it's unclear to me whether this is what he intends or just what I think. The boy has never thrown a tantrum. He's never slammed a door or said I-hate-you-you're-a-horrible-mother-I-wish-any-woman-was-my-mother-but-you! Without self-consciousness, he holds my hand as we walk through the parking lot. His hands are sticky no matter how many times I tell him to wash them.

Last night at dinner, I tried to comfort the boy. He had to write a paper about an event that took place on the date of his birth. He didn't like the assignment.

I'd done some research, and though the results weren't stand-up-and-cheer, I thought he might feel a little better. We were eating spaghetti when I told him Ron Howard's brother, Clint, was born on April 20. The siege on Londonderry, an exciting moment in British history, happened on April 20, and April 20 is also the date President Jimmy Carter was attacked by a swamp rabbit while on a canoe trip in Plains, Georgia. I encouraged the boy to think of his birthday as 4–20, which, as legend has it, is California cop code for public cannabis use. All the clocks in Quentin Tarantino's film *Pulp Fiction* are stopped at 4:20, and 4:20, I'm told, is teatime in Amsterdam. In fact, I said, as I passed him the Parmesan, since your favorite subject is social studies, you'll enjoy this: there's a subculture, an entire group of interesting people in places like, say, Ann Arbor, Michigan, or Boulder, Colorado, or Berkeley, California, who'd be thrilled to have April 20 as a birthday since it is also the day they celebrate an international event called the Hash Bash.

The boy thought about this. Then he stuck his pinky finger in the Parmesan. He sniffed it, sighing like a cynical and weary cop in a rumpled suit and fedora hat who's seen it all one too many times. He touched the tip of his pinky to his tongue. "It's marijuana, all right," he said. He was shaking his head like he regretted what he was about to say, but it was something that had to be said. "What we have here is a 4–20, and it's my own mother."

There are times when I can't help but take it personally, can't help but wonder if he would book his own mother on a misdemeanor parking violation, never mind felony drug charges; that he's out to get me, he'd stomp over my body to get at the last moldy heel of bread.

Then the T-ball mothers appear. A whole herd of them.

"Where's your hustle?" they ask.

"You gotta show some better hustle!" they shriek.

I don't own a pair of sweatpants, but that's what these women are wearing, and their hair is swept up in ponytails, each fastened with a bow. They've been planting perennials, but there's no dirt under their fingernails. They smell like vanilla and also like bleach.

They want to know where is my team spirit.

The boy does things I can't imagine and will never understand. Why spend hours constructing a diorama of *The Call of the Wild* and then forget to turn it in? Why score in the ninety-ninth percentile in the math section of your achievement test, then flunk math? Why eat three and a half pounds of crab legs during Red Lobster's all-you-can-eat crab leg promotion, then say you feel sick, that you're probably going to puke in the car on the ride home, but can we first stop at Toys "Я" Us? Was it because that old guy in the booth next to us nodded with such approval? I saw him give you a thumbs-up when the waitress brought out another pile. Is that why you did it?

The boy smiles. He shrugs. He says, I don't know.

Look, I tell the T-ball mothers. Childhood is oppressive. I determine what the boy's eating and when. I tell him when he's going to bed and when he can get up. I tell him when he can speak and when he must remain silent. There are certain things he's forbidden from ever saying, including *Not spaghetti again!* and *Dad would let me.*

But wouldn't you agree that motherhood is equally oppressive? Because of the boy, I can't drop fifty bucks on a pair of shoes. I can't fly to Paris on a moment's notice. I can't stay out all night. I can't even get liquored up when I need to.

The T-ball mothers join hands and sing. The tune is familiar but they've changed the words. "The bad mothers on the bus cry wah

wah wah." They smile and say, "Motherhood is a beautiful and sacred thing. You gotta go, go, go!"

My own mother used to say I was going to drive her to drink. When I was the boy's age, I did my Christmas shopping at Thrift Drugs, where I bought my mother a paperback copy of Christina Crawford's memoir, *Mommie Dearest*. That book would be made into a film in which Faye Dunaway, in the title role, rants and raves about how she doesn't much care for wire hangers.

The boy's clothes are in a heap on the floor, I tell the T-ball mothers, who in turn ask why I haven't hung up his clothes. "Don't you iron his clothes?" they ask. I don't even do his laundry. As soon as he was tall enough to reach the knobs, I showed him how to do his laundry. It's probably why he wanted to wear the same pair of socks day in and day out for twenty-eight days. I don't beat him, either. I don't spank him. My biggest, proudest accomplishment is that I've never even smacked his hand. When I tell the boy this—you're lucky, I tell him, my son—he says, "But you took that ten dollars away from me. Remember? We were walking to school that day, and I found ten dollars in the street, and you took it. Remember that?"

"No," I say. "I don't remember that. I don't have any idea what you're talking about."

Love in the Age of Ick

I once had a boyfriend who referred to me as his old lady. It was his adamant belief that while I already had a really sweet rack, gaining twenty-five pounds would make it even better. We were eating lunch at Taco Bell on the day he proposed: he had the kid behind the counter slip the ring into my bean burrito. I said yes. I'd known this guy for only eleven weeks, but already I was thinking about our future together: I was thinking about the best way to arrange furniture in a double-wide to maximize space, I was curious about what it would take to build a redwood deck, I was wondering if you could wallpaper over panel. "Anything you want, Momma," my fiancé said—he called me "Momma" and sometimes "Little Momma"—"You're the boss."

His name was Vincent Petrone. I met him at a smorgasbord called The Iron Ladle, where I spent the summer of 1989 bussing tables. He brought his grandma in for lunch one Sunday in June after Mass. She was a sweet-seeming lady with hair the color of old brick, bright pink lipstick, and powdery white skin. She was wearing a sweatshirt she'd fancied up herself—all it took was a BeDazzler, some black and gold metallic beads, and an iron-on transfer of a leopard. When I cleared away the first stack of dirty dishes from their booth, she said thank you, baby. When I cleared away the second, Vincent Petrone cleared his throat and said he could die happy now that he'd seen what heaven looks like. His grandma beamed at him, then asked didn't I think her grandson was a good-looking boy?

I said yes. I thought she was the cutest old lady I'd ever seen in her sparkly leopard sweatshirt, and I didn't want to hurt her feelings. But I was not telling the truth. Her grandson was not good-looking. His face was scarred. He wore black-rimmed glasses. He had a little moustache. There was an inky tattoo of a Maltese cross on his forearm, a naked mermaid on his biceps. He was wearing a yellow bowling shirt that had the word *Poocher* embroidered in red letters on the pocket. Under it, he wore a T-shirt that said *Twenty Ways to Say I Love You*. It showed stick figures engaged in twenty different sex acts. Those shirts heightened his *ick* factor, and I didn't yet know that he was twenty-nine years old, or that he was unemployed, or that he wore those shirts every day.

But something about him must have appealed to me because when he asked for my phone number, I gave it to him. I was refilling his grandma's cup of decaf when Vincent Petrone picked up his spoon, licked it, winked at me. "Momma, if you were my woman," he said, "you'd eat dessert every night."

I didn't yet know about Vincent's plans for fattening me up with the goal of increasing my rack, but from the look of his plate—chocolate soft-serve over chocolate pudding over many pieces of

chocolate cake—Vincent liked dessert. This charmed me. I immediately spun it into gold, I manipulated it into metaphor. This guy,
I decided, was a tragic hero, a misunderstood soul, the Bad Boy
who longed for something sweet.

I was nineteen years old, just arriving at that place some women
go to invent complex inner lives for a certain kind of man, one too
emotionally vulnerable to manage this kind of work on his own. I
would be a savior, a fixer, a social worker, because Vincent Petrone
needed me.

A drunk and a drunk driver, a habitual shoplifter, Vincent was
a guy who walked out of restaurants without paying; a guy who'd
fill his gas tank, then drive away; a guy who didn't leave a bar,
party, or parade without using his fists. I thought any little thing
he did that wasn't physically violent or illegal was endearing and
cute, evidence of my good influence and a good reason to stay the
course, see him through. He could've hot-wired that car, but he
didn't! He could've broken that guy's legs, but he didn't! He likes
coconut cream pie!

Less than a week after we first met, Vincent Petrone and I
decided we were in love, a couple, he would be my old man
and I would be his old lady. Though I told Vincent that I loved
him—I promised it, I swore it—I can't say I much liked him. But I
was nineteen and there were things *about* him that I liked.

I liked the scar on his face. He'd slid across asphalt in a motorcycle accident that left one side of his face normal, regular, a face
like everyone else's, and the other side forever bruised-looking. He
was self-conscious about his face and would lay his palm across his

cheek while talking to people. Whenever I saw him like that, I felt tenderly toward him.

But when he flipped off a mom at the red light next to us for looking at him funny, or when he flipped over his drink because he didn't like how the guy on the next bar stool over said hello to me—or when he raised a glass over his head then brought it down to shatter on the bar because he felt like no one was paying attention to what he was saying about his grandma's hip surgery when, in fact, he was so drunk and his words were so slurred that no one could understand what he was saying—I felt tired. Weary. Oh, Vincent, I'd say. I'd sigh, and my friends would want to know what are you doing with that loser?

I was enjoying the high drama of female masochism and martyrdom. I liked making excuses for Vincent—He's tired! He has a lot on his mind! He's had a hard life!—and I liked forgiving him. I forgave him for cheating, but accusing me of cheating. For stealing a hundred and fifty bucks out of my purse. For calling me a bitch slut whore, then crying about it, on his knees, his head pressed into my stomach, his arms wrapped around my waist. Oh, Momma, he'd say.

Oh please, my friends would say. How much more of this can you stand?

I liked when Vincent Petrone painted my name in curvy gold letters on the side of his demolition-derby car, a purple Dodge Dart. About thirty seconds into the event, the engine caught fire, but the metaphorical possibilities of that were something I had apparently overlooked.

I liked the white-trashiness of demolition derbies, the beery smells, the bright lipstick on the mouths of ladies in tight tapered jeans and spiky-heeled shoes, the crashing noise of men showing off for women. I liked thinking of myself as a Bad Boy's Girl: nice sweet shy demure good, the only kind of woman who could tame him, change him, who could make him true, who could, someday, possibly even make him act right.

A year before I met Vincent Petrone, I'd hit the streets, knocking on doors and handing out pamphlets that listed reasons one should vote for then vice president George Bush. I did it because I had a crush on a Young Republican, a clean-shaven boy in khaki pants, navy blue polo shirt, and tasseled loafers. To win his affection, I saved up for a Laura Ashley dress, I pulled my hair back with a headband, I painted my nails a tasteful, ladylike pale pink. I wore panty hose. Heels and perfume. I pledged a sorority my freshman year of college.

But after all my attempts to be who he wanted me to be, the Young Republican still asked some other girl, a girl named Ashleigh who had a whole closet full of Laura Ashley dresses, to his fraternity formal. I didn't believe for a minute that he loved her. I thought he had taken up with Ashleigh only to please his father. I'd never met the man, but I imagined him as a cardigan-wearing, pipe-smoking, emotionally distant CEO hell-bent on marrying his son to the daughter of a likewise powerful man as a way to increase his fortune, like the wealthy patriarchs I'd seen on *The Young and the Restless* and *Guiding Light*.

Now that I was Vincent Petrone's old lady, I could throw away my headbands and perm my hair. I could make it even bigger by blow-drying it upside down, teasing it out and up, and spraying it stiff with Aqua Net. I could peg my jeans. I could wear blue eyeliner. After work, I sat in Vincent's apartment getting high. Marijuana gave me a bad case of the munchies, and I had trouble resisting the Double Stuf Oreos Vincent pushed on me. Double Stuf means Double D, he'd sing. We listened to Bon Jovi or Guns N' Roses or Warrant or Poison or Mötley Crüe or Def Leppard while I dunked Oreos into skim milk. I attempted to give myself blond highlights with hydrogen peroxide but ended up with orange streaks. I wrote long earnest soulful entries in my journal about all the phony people in the world, about how being Vincent Petrone's woman meant I was more real, more authentic than a girl named Ashleigh could ever hope to be.

I also liked that a girl like Ashleigh—a girl who wore floral-print dresses and bows in her hair, a girl who probably had 1,000-thread count sheets and knew when and how to curtsey—would not, could not, did not, have what it takes to handle a guy like Vincent Petrone, one a little mean and a little violent, a little controlling and a little crazy.

But I could. I did. It was a choice I had made.

Vincent Petrone was not a Republican. Or a Democrat. He didn't vote. He dropped out of high school, earned a GED, he didn't go to college. He told me that when he was little, he'd wanted to be an astronaut, but he otherwise didn't talk about his dreams. He'd been in jail in Florida, but was vague about why. He didn't talk about his mother except to say she moved to Florida when he was eight. He was clear about his feelings for his father— he hated the man—but wouldn't elaborate on why. He was unwilling to talk about so many things that I could only imagine the worst: a childhood of thrift-store back-to-school clothes and forgotten birthdays; of free school lunches and no-name tennis shoes; of no money to correct bad teeth, no money for trombone lessons or ski trips; of nothing but socks and underwear under the Christmas tree. I made Vincent Petrone into the poster boy for "Troubled Past" or "Sad Childhood" or "Dysfunctional Family." I tried to make it up to him. I bought him packs of Marlboros. I felt sorry for him, and I called it love.

There were things Vincent Petrone loved: his grandma who raised him and Neil Young, puppies and babies, the way air smells before a storm, and yellow kitchens—Vincent thought all kitchens should be yellow, like his grandma's. Every morning he drove his grandma to Mass, waiting for her in the car while he nipped bourbon or smoked a joint to calm his shakes while drumming his fingers against the steering wheel to *Everybody Knows This Is Nowhere*. In the afternoon, he ate whatever she fixed him for lunch, then worked on his demolition-derby car, my name glinting gold in the sun.

He spent his evenings keeping tabs on me. By July, he'd become more insistent about wanting to know where I was, who I was with, and where I was going. He appreciated how I looked in short skirts, tight shirts, and blue eyeliner, but any male attention that came my way because of it peeved him. It made him mad if I joked around with male coworkers or chatted with male customers at The Iron Ladle. The night manager there didn't like the way Vincent loomed around the smorgasbord in a menacing way, watching me work, staring down anyone who met his eye. He'd say what are you looking at? He'd say take a picture, it lasts longer. He'd say you got something you wanna say to me? When the night manager told him he couldn't hang out there anymore, he keyed her car. The next day she told me she didn't need me anymore, she'd taken my name off the schedule.

Take care, she said, and good luck.

Later that night, back at his apartment, Vincent Petrone poured a fifth of whiskey and five cans of Miller Genuine Draft down the drain. He said he was drying out. He said he was doing it just for me. I'd better know the sacrifice he was making, he said, and I assured him I knew, I did.

Three days later we went to a Legends of Rock concert outside Cleveland where Vincent Petrone got snookered. He took off his *Twenty Ways to Say I Love You* T-shirt and waved it like a flag over his head. He snorted some cocaine, he smoked some dope, he swilled some bourbon. He swayed as Blue Öyster Cult played "Burnin' for You," and he pumped his fist and shouted yeah yeah yeah as Molly Hatchet played "Flirtin' with Disaster." He introduced me to a girl named Sheila and said we were going to have a threesome in the car, he introduced me to a girl named Janice and said we were going to have a foursome in the parking lot, he introduced me to a leather-clad biker chick named Willa and said he and she had fucked behind the port-a-potties. Oh, Vincent! I said each time. Oh, Vincent!

On the way home, he wove all over the highway, onto the shoulder, then across the white lines, and I don't suppose his ability to concentrate on keeping the car on the road was helped by my shrieking. Vincent! Oh, Vincent! I had it in my head that I could do a better job keeping us on the road, a better job keeping us out of jail should a cop pull us over. To demonstrate my steady hand and excellent judgment, I tried to squeeze myself between Vincent and the steering wheel. I tried to grab control of the steering wheel, but he tried to jerk it away from me. We swerved in front of a semi that honked its horn and flashed its lights at a rhythm that matched my pounding heart. That did not help me stop shrieking, I could not seem to stop.

Then he raised his hand to me, and that's when all the things I liked about him turned into all the things I hated about myself. As soon as he raised his hand to me, I knew exactly how much I could stand.

I bit Vincent Petrone.

I bit him on the arm, like I was a dog or a toddler or a near-sighted vampire. I broke skin, I drew blood, I left marks. It caught us both off guard. I stopped shrieking. Vincent pulled over to the side of the highway. It was the middle of the night, a beautiful warm starry night in late August. We were somewhere in Ohio. He said get out; I got out.

A few days later, Vincent's grandma came to see me. She brought me a present, a shoe box containing many pairs of long dangly earrings, earrings like chandeliers, like jellyfish and fishing lures. She said she'd been buying them up with the intention of giving them to me for Christmas. She said her grandson was quite a handful and always had been. She wanted me to understand that Vincent had a hard life, a sad life, full of disappointment and sorrow. It's why he acted up sometimes. She said she hoped I could help him. We'll do it together, she said, you and me, we'll help him straighten out. She wanted me to call Vincent, to tell him I was sorry. I think the two of you are so good for each other, she said. Promise me you'll call him.

I promised I would.

I was lying.

I never saw Vincent Petrone again, I never spoke to him, I never heard from him.

Instead, he became a story I'd tell over strawberry margaritas, the same story any number of women can tell, the one that's sometimes called What Was I Thinking? or Back When I Was in My Ick Phase. I found he was a lot more fun to talk about than he'd ever been to live with; I discovered a lot of women had Vincents of their own.

But every once in a while, without my permission and against my will, this man shows up in my dreams, wearing his *Poocher* shirt, driving his purple demolition-derby car, my name glinting gold in the sun. He says he has something to say to me. He wants to know who do I think I am. He wants to know did I really love him or did I just hate myself. He wants to remind me of the girl I used to be.

What's (Not) Simple

Dogs love Karl Bennett. When dogs see him, they quiver and flail, they wiggle and whine. They throw themselves at his feet, showing him their soft bellies, stretching out their necks.

My dog especially loves Karl Bennett. A border collie–German shepherd mix, my dog terrorizes most people, but when Karl's white pickup pulls into my driveway, Bobby's tail wags hard, his tongue lolls, his lips curl into a goofy smile. Just this morning, Bobby strained at his leash, attempting to get to the passenger's seat of Karl's truck. Bobby wanted to lick Karl's face, his hand, his boots.

But when Karl flicked a cigarette lighter at him and told him to go lay down, Bobby, in a fit of obedience quite unlike him, obeyed. Bobby's enthusiasm for this man irritates me. Because Karl Bennett is my ex-husband, my dog's attitude seems disloyal.

. . .

Karl Bennett isn't tall. He stands about five-feet-seven; his chest is broad; his hair, once dark, is now a wispy gray. He's a sweet-looking guy, handsome, with green eyes and bushy eyebrows and a neatly trimmed moustache. During hunting season, he grows a beard.

Karl Bennett doesn't like to see people cooing at their dogs or murmuring sweet nothings into their floppy ears. When he pets my dog, Karl extends one finger and touches, just barely, along the top of Bobby's head. Karl doesn't like for people to sleep with their dogs. He doesn't like knowing we put our cereal bowls or dinner plates on the floor so our dogs can lap up the remaining milk or tongue off the bit of mashed potatoes and gravy we saved just for them. Karl Bennett doesn't like dogs in the house, period.

When I want to annoy him, I tell Karl that I fried up four eggs for breakfast: two for me, two for Bobby. When I want to disgust him, I tell him how I believe Bobby's emotional problems stem from his being taken from his mama at too young an age. "Bobby suffers from separation anxiety," I say.

When I'm really looking to get on Karl's nerves, I coo at my dog, asking him does he love his uncle Karl. "You're simple," Karl says. "You're simple in the head."

There are other things Karl doesn't like. Angela Lansbury is one. For reasons he cannot explain, Karl intensely dislikes Angela Lansbury. If he hears her voice or even a voice that sounds like hers on television, he changes the channel. Karl doesn't much care for Hillary Clinton, either, but he believes the reasons for this should be obvious, and thus require no explanation.

More than once, Karl Bennett has informed me that he doesn't hate women. He may believe that women can be spiteful, yes, and they can also be sneaky and shrill. According to Karl Bennett, women are frequently impulsive, manipulative, underhanded, untrustworthy, fickle, impossible to please, confusing on purpose, and full of contradictions, but he doesn't hate women.

"Quit asking me if I hate women," he says.

When he was seventeen years old, Karl Bennett lost his virginity to a gorilla girl. It happened the summer he spent working the saltwater-taffy booth with the traveling carnival, and since then women have played an important role in his life. Karl Bennett has found jobs and quit jobs because of a woman, he's built houses and bought houses and sold houses because of a woman. He's started his life over from scratch, and he's made and kept promises, and more than once, because of a woman, Karl Bennett has been disappointed, despairing, heartsick.

He's been married three times to three different women, and he has three children, a daughter and two sons, nineteen years separating the oldest from the youngest.

Though his freezer is full of elk and mule deer, Karl does, on occasion, have salted peanuts for supper. Sometimes, he'll pull open a tin of sardines. Sometimes, you can talk him into turning down the television and playing a hand of rummy. Karl has just turned fifty-three, and the last few years have been the longest stretch he's ever lived alone. He says he's come to prefer it.

Karl Bennett can't hold his liquor. Scotch makes him mean. He faints at the sight of his own blood. He's never surfed the Internet and he doesn't own a dictionary. He doesn't have a suit, he doesn't have a passport. Karl Bennett doesn't like looking up numbers in the phone book. He doesn't like Ed Bradley's pierced ear, women who wear a lot of makeup, or little boys with long hair.

Once, after we staggered into a gas station after last call, Karl Bennett stumbled up to the counter with at least two dozen individually wrapped condoms. The lady at the register said, "You may be good, but you ain't that good."

There have been several dogs in Karl's life. There was a red heeler named Jingles. There was Butch, the Yorkie he had with Ex-Wife Number One, and Bandit, the beagle he had with Ex-Wife Number Two. Over the course of our marriage, Karl and I had two dogs: both red heelers, both named Jack. When Karl was twelve years old, he had a dog named Sandy, some mangy muttly thing that he loved a lot. The problem with Sandy, though, was that she had a taste for the neighbor's chickens. After she'd killed one too many, Karl's father told him a chicken-killing dog is only good dead, then handed over the .22. "You know what you need to do," the old man said, and Karl did what the old man wanted: he took Sandy into the woods and shot her, but he had neither the heart nor the stomach to bury her. The next morning, Karl found Sandy alive, but barely, crawling out from under the porch to lick his hand. To this day, Karl Bennett believes that's an example of love, pure and true.

Out of all his sad stories—and Karl has quite a few—the story about Sandy is, for me, the saddest. I remember the first time I heard it, early on in our courtship: how Karl kept his head down, his hands fidgeting with something in his lap—a piece of twine, maybe, or a twig. His voice was soft, but flat, his brow furrowed.

I felt so bad for him. Looking back, I don't think Karl Bennett told that story to seduce me, though that was the effect it had.

W hen I first met Karl Bennett, he and his red heeler, Jingles, lived on forty-three acres in western Pennsylvania, land he was just about to lose in the divorce settlement with Ex-Wife Number Two. His house was pretty much a shack, but with help from the Amish, he'd built a beautiful barn for his Appaloosas. Karl stretched a hose from the barn and through the window in the shack's bathroom to fill the toilet with enough water to flush it. Squirrels nested in his attic. His refrigerator held beer, pepperoni, and jugs of milk in various stages of souring. He took his laundry to his mother. Karl drove a red pickup then, and Jingles rode shotgun, growling at everyone everywhere they went.

Karl Bennett has a friendly smile. If you saw him standing in front of the freezer section at the grocery store contemplating ice cream or standing in line at the convenience store to pay for his gas and buy a scratch-off lottery ticket, you wouldn't feel shy about saying hello. I've seen women give him sidelong glances; I've seen women bite down on their lips to redden them, fluff out their hair, and widen their eyes as they moved past him.

"No one can say any of my wives were ugly women," Karl says. "At least not when I married them."

Ex-Wives Number One and Number Two still live in western Pennsylvania, and as Karl tells it, they like to call each other up and swap stories about him. Neither of them has ever called me.

Karl Bennett and I both live in western Colorado, where we moved in 1996, separated in 1997, tormented each other in 1998, and officially divorced in 1999. I live in Grand Junction, in a house on Main Street; I live with the son Karl and I share custody of; and the man the State of Colorado says is my common-law husband; and of course, Bobby, my dog.

Karl lives just outside town in a shabby little duplex that doesn't allow dogs. Once a month, when his child support check is due, Karl Bennett tells me he's broke or something close to it. No woman in his life, no dog, no money, Karl also doesn't have health insurance. He hasn't gone to the dentist in some twenty-odd years, but even when he had insurance that included dental, he never got around to going, and though he's a drinker of coffee (cups and cups, all day long, each with a splash of cream)—and though he's a smoker of cigarettes (Salem Lights, a pack a day, sometimes less, but more often more) and he's an eater of junk food, especially sweets (I once watched him do a shot of maple syrup)—Karl Bennett's teeth are beautiful, immaculate: white, straight, his own. His arms are long. "Monkey arms," he says, "buggy-whip arms." Karl Bennett is long-backed and short-waisted; he has no butt. It's hard to find pants that fit him. Karl Bennett has a solid-looking belly pushing over the top of his jeans, and he has a lockbox containing family photos and spare keys that unlocked pickups he used to drive and doors to places he used to live. Our son tells me there are bars of gold in that box—Karl confirmed this, though he's vague about how much—bought during the Y2K scare.

At one time, there were photos of a woman in that box, one of Karl's ex-girlfriends. They were naked photos. Back when I knew where Karl kept the keys to that box, I came across those photos, I wrote a nasty note, something about here's some trash that looks like you, I stuck the note and the photos in an envelope, and I mailed them to her.

. . .

When he graduated from high school, Karl Bennett was almost twenty years old. He wasn't stupid—staying in school was a good way to avoid the draft—but he also just didn't like school, preferring to play hooky, sometimes with his buddies, who were in fact stupid, but more often by himself. Karl liked to hunt and fish and sit in the woods eating the egg salad sandwiches his mother had packed for his lunches. He daydreamed about what most kids in rural western Pennsylvania daydream about: leaving.

He came close to not graduating. The only reason he did was because he and his mother and the principal of Laurel High reached an understanding: Karl would show up to school every day during the last three months of his senior year and he'd take two swats every morning before homeroom. His high school commencement was in June 1970—a month before I was born.

Even back then, in 1970, Karl Bennett was thinking about the places where a man could live off the land, off the grid, with a woman and some kids, away from cities and their people and noise. Places with no telephones. The barter system. Wild places where the sky is big and the mountains are big and the nearest neighbor is miles and miles away. Western places where a man could build a toolshed without a permit from the government giving him permission or dig a hole in the ground and call it a toilet.

But nineteen years later, Karl Bennett was still in western Pennsylvania. I was a sophomore in college, waitressing in this little diner where Karl, recently divorced from Number Two, came every morning for breakfast (a ham-and-cheese omelet and whole-wheat toast) and every afternoon for lunch (a cheeseburger with lettuce, mayo on the side).

Karl Bennett never tapped his spoon against his coffee cup when he wanted a warm-up. He didn't blow his nose, then leave wet Kleenex scattered across the table. Karl Bennett was not one of the men who wiggled a finger at me, then after I walked over, coffeepot in hand, said, "I just wanted to see if this finger could make you come." Unlike the other men—old farmers, a veterinarian, a blacksmith, a physician, and a shareholder in Heinz, all of whom were perverts—Karl Bennett was a gentleman. He was patient when the diner was busy, empathetic when other customers were assholes. He was a generous tipper, never leaving less than twenty percent.

What wooed me was the pretty way Karl talked about the places he daydreamed about. He brought in his Rand McNally atlas and traced his finger along those places: Montana, the Dakotas, Wyoming, Colorado. (At the time, I was taking French Lit, where I read about Emma Bovary doing the same sort of thing with a map of Paris.) Karl especially liked the places on the map that weren't rashed with little red population dots. He described the cozy little log cabin he planned to build; did I think it should have a wraparound porch? I did.

"Then we'll have one," he said.

We could have horses, he said, and chickens. We could have dogs. We'd never have to chain them to a stake, and they could nap on the porch next to our rocking chairs. Karl said something about how we'd snowshoe into the woods and saw down our very own Christmas tree. He mentioned something about rigging up a clothesline in the yard so we could let our bedsheets dry in the sun. He held my hand under the table and told me I was pretty. He said words like "paradise" and "fresh start" and "new beginning."

I knew this guy was twenty years older than me. I knew he was twice divorced, and I'd heard his ex-wives hated him passionately. I knew his daughter was three years younger than me. I knew he lived in a dump, and I sort of suspected he had some weird ideas about what a woman's place might be. After hearing the sad story of Sandy the dog, I should have guessed that Karl Bennett had some screwed-up ideas about love.

Karl Bennett spent years working as a logger. He's worked the woods; he's owned a skidder, a loader, a dump truck, a pallet shop. He can eyeball a tree and tell you how many board feet it has. He can whittle a block of wood into a jewelry box; he can conjure a nightstand out of a stump. He snaps his fingers and that shabby old desk you would've chopped into firewood becomes beautiful. Here in Grand Junction, Karl is the foreman of a sawmill, overseeing a crew that includes men with felony convictions and Mexicans without green cards. The ex-cons aren't worth a shit, Karl says. The ex-cons are simple, and for Karl Bennett, simple is the worst thing a person can be. Simple means lacking good common sense, but it also applies to people who are obtuse, stubborn, or illogical. Simple people are those unwilling to accept or unable to recognize that their intelligence has limits.

But most often, simple means you have no claim to dignity. For example, an ex-convict who slices off his own finger because he's too busy giggling about the wonders of eating pussy to pay attention to his finger's proximity to the saw blade is being simple. But it's not the man's carelessness alone that makes him that way. An accident can happen to anyone. It's that the man was giggling about pussy-eating when it happened.

The Mexicans are not simple. Karl likes and respects the Mexicans: they put in a hard day, they don't bother anyone. Karl doesn't speak Spanish, and it's fun to hear him say their names: José, Ernesto, Juan, Jesús. It's fun to see them smile and nod while Karl Bennett rants about how trees are our only renewable natural resource. Karl doesn't think much of Earth First!ers and Mother Earthers. "The toilet paper they use to wipe their ass?" he says. "Where do they think that comes from?" Karl can talk about God's green earth in a way that doesn't sound dopey. Though his politics are undeniably liberal—he's all for labor unions and a woman's right to choose, paying schoolteachers what they're worth and taking care of old people and the poor—Karl Bennett votes Republican. He says it's because the Republicans get it: trees are our only renewable natural resource.

But it's also because Karl Bennett is a supporter of the NRA, a payer of its dues, a believer in its mission, and a buyer of its collectible commemorative coins.

On January 25, 1992, in Wampum, Pennsylvania, I married Karl Bennett. Held at Pauline Isaac's Wedding Chapel and Motel, our wedding was a small ceremony, just the four of us: me, Karl, the preacher, and the preacher's wife. I was six months pregnant.

Afterward, we went to his mother's house and ate pot roast

with carrots, celery, and potatoes. Karl Bennett seemed happy. "We'll make it," he said. "For better or for worse."

I was a prudish pregnant woman, and as far as I was concerned, a traditional wedding night was out of the question, and anyway, Karl was tired. "Sleep well, Mrs. Bennett," he said.

But I was wide-awake. We lived so far out of town that we couldn't get cable, so my television-watching choices were limited. I remember *The Best Little Whorehouse in Texas* was on at three that morning. I remember watching an infomercial for the Incredible Sweater Machine, and an infomercial where Cher was hyping some anti-wrinkle cream. There was also one about a device that cut hair: the clippers were somehow attached to a vacuum cleaner, making the hair-cutting process tidy.

Karl woke up for that one; he said he'd had that same idea twelve years before, and he told me about another idea he had. Did I realize that a man has these bones in his shoulders that prevent him from getting lotion on his back? A woman, though, doesn't have that problem. A woman can get lotion on her back unaided. But what if you got one of those paint rollers with a hollow tube handle, you filled it with lotion—"Cocoa butter, vanilla, aloe, whatever you like," he said—and you attach it to the bathroom wall, you press a button, and the man just stands against it.

"I can put lotion on your back for you," I told him.

He said he would appreciate it, and in that moment, I thought maybe this marriage could work.

Later, I wouldn't be so sure. Karl Bennett was rolling down the window in his pickup, he was pulling one of our baby's dirty diapers out of a plastic bag. He was going to hurl it out the window and over the top of the truck and into the neighbor's yard. He did this because the neighbor shot Karl's dog Jingles three years before, and Karl Bennett can hold a grudge. Every time we went out, we drove past this particular neighbor's so Karl could throw a dirty diaper into this guy's yard. I don't know what Karl planned to do once we had our son toilet-trained, though it wouldn't really matter. We'd be separated by then.

From the outside, where Karl Bennett lives looks like the residence of any normal person: a driveway, some green grass, a front door.

Inside, in Karl Bennett's living room, four deer heads hang mounted on the walls. There is an assortment of animal skulls bleached white from the sun, that he found while hunting and hiking over the years, rowed neatly across his mantel. There are animal bones; he told me one is a mule deer's pecker bone. There are skins: deer hides and a black bear's coat, the result of a hunting trip in Alaska. Its head is still attached and my dog Bobby eyeballs it with some anxiety and barks at it nervously. If you tell Karl his living room looks like a killing field, he's defensive. If you tell him it's lucky the two of you are divorced, because there's no way in hell you'd accept such a living room, he's hurt.

"It wouldn't look like this if you were here," he'd say.

The last year we were a couple was our first year in Grand Junction. Karl Bennett and I fought, often and a lot. We fought loudly enough that the cops came. We fought silently, sleeping in separate rooms and ignoring each other when we passed in the kitchen. We fought about money—our lack of it. Karl reminded me I was the one who said money can't buy happiness.

We fought about things that happened years before: how those naked pictures of his ex-girlfriend came to be mailed back to her, for example. Apparently, she'd been upset and called her attorney, who called Karl's attorney, who called Karl. When my involvement came into question, I denied everything, but Karl knew better.

"You're simple," he said. "That was a simple thing to do."

We fought about Jingles, shot and killed by the neighbor; Karl's fault, I thought, for allowing the dog to run loose. We fought about why we gave away Jack Dog Number One: I didn't trust him around the baby. We fought about why we gave away Jack Dog Number Two: off the leash, he bit a guy. We fought about the mean, horrible things Karl Bennett had said that I still remembered even if he didn't, and we fought about the mean, horrible things he was sure I must've said even if he couldn't remember what they were. When I pointed out that everything wrong was his fault because he was the one who said, "I'm moving to Colorado with or without you," Karl said I was the fool who believed him.

We fought about how much I hated western Colorado, the unbearable desert heat, the bizarre canyon landscape, the rednecks in pickups with gun racks who hooted at me as I walked down North Avenue. We fought about the fact that the closest woods where he could find work were in Utah's La Sal Mountains, too far away to commute, so Karl lived there, in a tent on the job site, a little too contentedly, coming home only on weekends. We fought about if I was happy to see him when he came home on weekends. We fought about his growing suspicions concerning the man who would become, according to Colorado state law, my common-law husband, and we also spent a great deal of time fighting about which one of us was simple.

. . .

Karl would tell you that from the first moment he laid eyes on every one of his wives, he never once took notice of, or even for a moment fantasized about, another woman, not even a supermodel or movie star. He's told me that, and though I pooh-poohed it, saying that it seems a little unbelievable, not to mention unhealthy, I really do believe him. When Karl Bennett tells his wife she's the most beautiful girl in the world, when he holds her hand and says to her for-better-or-for-worse, he means it. Things just don't always work out the way we mean.

I harbor grudges against Karl Bennett. There is my bad credit, for example, and that getting involved with him meant my father wouldn't speak to me for almost a year, the old man literally turning his back when I stepped into my parents' house. There's also the rice steamer my uncle gave us for Christmas in '95 that I know Karl took when he moved out.

But I owe Karl Bennett. He replaced the brakes on my truck; when I broke down in traffic last week, he was the one I called. When I wanted mulch for my garden, he brought me bags and bags of it from the sawmill. When we go out of town, I don't have to kennel my dog: Bobby goes and stays with his uncle Karl. When our son is behaving in ways that I find especially obnoxious, Karl Bennett is the only one I don't get pissed at for agreeing.

I will always admire the things Karl Bennett knows: how to skin a buck, break a horse, sew a button. He knows that duct tape, WD-40, and Neosporin are the only emergency supplies you'll ever need. He knew that when his father died, he wouldn't have much to say, and that when his mother died, he'd weep. Karl Bennett knows he doesn't do well in a crowd, but one-on-one, he can be quite charming.

Once I got it in my head that I wanted a dog, there was no changing my mind. My son and Al, my common-law husband, and I had been living together for not quite a year, and since I'm set firm on no more babies, it seemed to me that what the three of us needed to bond as a familial unit was a dog.

I got us Bobby.

But my son and Bobby didn't connect as I'd hoped. Bobby was high-strung and high-maintenance and he had alpha issues. Bobby was a very destructive, very humpy puppy. Bobby was a hairball with sharp teeth. It was during a weekend with his father, a Friday night, that the boy admitted to hating all dogs in principle and Bobby in particular, and for Karl Bennett, a boy who hates dogs is an example of tragedy, pure and true.

On Sunday, when the boy returned to my house, he was carrying a large wicker basket. In that basket, there sat a tiny trembling black puppy, a sweet, cute puppy, some kind of Yorkie-poodle mix, no bigger than a grapefruit, with curly hair, shiny black eyes, and a teeny pink tongue.

Karl Bennett is lucky he wasn't standing in my living room that Sunday night. He wasn't there to see his son cradling one puppy while fending off the humpy advances of another. He wasn't there to hear me, Ex-Wife Number Three, explain—gently at first, then more vigorously—that we would not/could not have a second puppy.

It's lucky because Karl Bennett is not crazy about sobbing children or heartbroken children or his own child's sadness. Karl is a softy for children, and he will invent ways to make them feel better.

He can't much deal with furious women, either; he says one thing he knows for sure is that a furious woman ought be avoided.

Sometimes Karl knows how to act, and sometimes he doesn't. On my twentieth birthday, he sent me two dozen long-stemmed red roses. On my twenty-first birthday, we conceived our son. On my twenty-second birthday, he gave me a set of four green plastic cereal bowls.

My ex-husband also knows that some things are never simple. That Sunday night he backed that white pickup of his out of my driveway fast, even before our son and that puppy-in-a-basket came through the front door. Karl Bennett hightailed it out of there before anyone could accuse him of any wrongdoing—impulsive, manipulative, or otherwise—and that night, all night, when his phone rang and rang and rang, he didn't answer it.

My Abel Brother

Growing up in my house, there were the things a boy did: Mow the lawn. Take out the trash. Be home by breakfast, and grunt when asked how was the movie he supposedly saw.

There were the things a nice young lady did: Wash the dishes. Fold the laundry. Be home before midnight, and submit to a timed exam in which she correctly answered specific questions concerning the minute details of the plot, characters, and setting of the movie she supposedly saw, in order to prove she didn't skip said movie to hang out in the park smoking cigarettes, drinking beer, shooting heroin between her toes, and/or having sex with some grungy, zitty boy, thus ending up pregnant and/or diseased, not to mention disgraced and scandalized.

All questions must be answered promptly, no dawdling. All answers must be in blue or black ink, legible handwriting and properly spelled. No looking at the ceiling. You won't find any answers on the ceiling. Are you ready? Go!

Question Number One: Name the film's costume designer. Question Number Two: Name the film's Toronto caterer. And here's a hint: Think carefully before you answer. I wouldn't want you to confuse the Toronto caterer with the New York caterer. Question Number Three...What do you mean you're still thinking about the first question? All right. Tell me the truth. Out with it. Did you or did you not see this movie? Well? Tell me the truth. Where did you really go, and who were you really with?

While my brothers did the things boys were supposed to do—while they arm wrestled and Indian wrestled and thumb wrestled, while they pushed the coffee table out of the way so they could wrestle like puppies on the living room floor, while they hunted and fished, played high school football then college, while they mowed the lawn and shoveled the snow, while they worked their asses off at my father's auto body shop after school and all day every day during the summer from fifth grade through graduation—I did the things a girl does. I improved my posture by gliding across the room with a dictionary balanced on top of my head. I was a Brownie, then a Girl Scout (the first meeting after cookie sales ended, the troop leader measured our waists, and we had to pay a dime for every inch we gained eating all those Thin Mints, all those Samoas). I counted calories, which meant I struggled with math. I babysat younger kids because, as everyone knows, a girl with younger siblings should be really good with kids. I set the supper table and cleared the supper table, loaded and emptied the dishwasher, scrubbed the toilet. I sprayed shirts and pants and my father's white handkerchiefs with starch, then ironed these things wrinkle-free. My after-school job was shelving books at the public library. For recreation, I called up one of my girlfriends and said catty things about another.

It wasn't until after I was grown, after I had a son of my own, that it seemed important to change my ideas about maleness, masculinity. I wanted to raise my son differently, outside the perimeters of such rigid and outdated gender roles.

To make this happen, I gave my son a doll, brown-eyed and brown-haired, a boy doll—"This is *your* baby!" I told him—and I suggested my son name his doll. I said he could, if he wanted, cuddle it and rock it to sleep. I encouraged him to love and nurture it.

Further, for every book I read him that featured a male protagonist, I read him one that featured a girl. I also forbade him from playing with toy guns, I created a safe space where he could feel free to talk about his feelings, and I dressed him like Little Lord Fauntleroy. On his first Christmas, I clothed him in black velvet knickers, a white blouse, black-and-white-checked suspenders, a black velvet bow tie, white knee socks, black leather shoes, and a little black velvet beret. He looked adorable, and I was proud to be doing my part in bringing up a sweeter, gentler, dandier generation of boy.

Only it didn't work. It wouldn't take. My son didn't want to hug and kiss his baby. He wanted to crush its head by running over it with a dump truck. His final analysis of *Little Women* was that Jo March and her sisters were silly, boring, and stupid. He bit his toast into the shape of a pistol and pointed it at me. "Pow!" he said. "Bang! Bang! You're dead."

When I asked him how it made him feel to do that, to bite his toast into a weapon, to point that weapon at the woman who gave him life, and to, paradoxically, metaphorically, destroy that same woman's life, he said it made him feel like he wanted more toast.

My son was in first grade when he and I went to a backyard

birthday party where six-year-old boys were taking off their shirts, then thumping their chests like they were the feral sons of Tarzan. One boy whirled his shirt in a circle over his head as though he was about to lasso a wild mustang, while the others hooted and hollered and hissed. One boy pushed his belly out as far as he could, then scratched it; another boy burped. My son was the one grunting and flexing his biceps, baring and clenching his teeth. A bouquet of helium balloons tied to a tree floated above the shirtless boys, and some of them jumped up and down, like primitives, yipping and screeching and poking at it with sticks.

A few minutes later, they were shaking cans of pop, which they then quickly buried in the sandbox before scurrying away. One of the other mothers there said what on earth are those little dickens up to?

Because I grew up with brothers, it was obvious to me what they were up to. They were building bombs out of vigorously shaken carbonated cola. They were anticipating a really awesome sandbox explosion that would morph into the sandstorm of the century at any minute. They were running for their lives.

"Run!" they implored us. "Seek shelter! It's gonna blow!"

As the oldest child, the only daughter, I've watched boys blow things up and shoot things and skin things and set things on fire. I've seen them scratch at their bellies, their butts, their balls. I've heard each boast that he's the fastest, the strongest, the smartest, the very best. I've heard them say Butthead. Dickhead. Fuckwad. Douche Breath. That Christmas I dressed my son in the black velvet knickers, the black velvet bow tie, the white blouse, the black-and-white-checked suspenders, my brothers removed the outfit and wouldn't give it back, not even the white knee socks or the black leather shoes or the black velvet beret, forcing the boy to spend his first major holiday naked but for his diaper. On more than one occasion, one of my brothers has squeezed me in a headlock, forcing me to smell his armpit, his fart, his foul breath, then asking, "How do you like my new perfume?"

More than once, I've wondered who I would have been if I'd had a sister. What would my life have been like? How would it have been different? Because I think there would be differences. I think I would be less entertained by belching, but I would also have made better choices about my hair. A sister would have taken me aside and said it's not 1988, you're over thirty, it's time to invest in a flatiron and grow out those puffy bangs.

I was three years old when my brother Mitchell was born, and I don't have an early memory that doesn't include him. In fact, he is my first memory. I'm standing on my tiptoes, peering into his bassinet, and our father is asking me who's that? Because I am not thrilled with the sudden existence of this baby brother I'm told I need to love and be nice to, I refuse to dignify my father's question with a response. Who's that? What do you mean who's that? Who is what?

But as Mitchell got older, I learned how handy it was to have him around. I stopped thinking of my little brother as a curse and started seeing him as the greatest gift my parents ever could have given me, that special little something every girl needs: a scapegoat of her very own, someone upon whom a girl can pin her crimes. Mitchell and I were adults before I finally revealed that I, not he, was the one who flushed that apple down the toilet. My brother, who'd received a couple pretty good stripes across the butt because of this incident, said no kidding, really, and all this time I thought it was me. Bitch.

Of the three of us, my brother Mitchell was the perfect one. Mitchell was who adults had in mind when they uttered words like "good boy," "nice kid," "gifted and talented student," and "Have you ever considered getting him into child modeling?" Ladies young and old approached him in parking lots, in grocery stores, at the bank, on the street. They might have tightened their lips into a pinched-up smile at me, a loud and show-offy little girl with scabby knees, bitten-down nails, and gnawed-on cuticles, but even the most ardent believers in zero population growth went goo-goo-ga-ga at the sight of my brother. They held Mitchell's little face between their hands and gazed into his very big, very blue eyes fringed by very thick, very long lashes. They got all aflutter over his rosebud lips and sweet, sweet smile. They wanted to tou-sle his silky hair and squeeze his pink cheeks.

"Oh, what eyelashes!" they'd exclaim.

"Oh, it's always the boys, isn't it, blessed with such eyelashes!"

"Oh," they'd cry. "He's so cute-handsome-good-sweet-wonderful-brilliant-adorable-fantastic-fabulous. . . ."

At some point their voices would blur and their words would blur, and I'd chew on my cuticles until what I heard spewing out of their black-holes-for-mouths sounded more like fucking-bratty-monster-stupid-pig-guts-baboon-testicles-bastard-son-of-a-bitch because by this point even our mother was getting in on the act. "Oh, I know," she'd sigh, because being the mother of the New Messiah was such a burden. "I really should think about getting him into child modeling."

In retrospect, it wasn't Mitchell's fault. Though he was asthmatic and living in a house with a smoker unaware that smoking aggravates asthma, though he was allergic to smoke and dust and mold and everything else in the world—though he got sick on roller coasters like The Spider, the kind of ride that whirls you round and round and up and down, causing my brother to puke up hot dogs and blue cotton candy on the people waiting in line below—Mitchell was an extraordinarily good-looking kid.

He was also dreamy and smart in a way that adults like, learning the names of stars, of insects, of dinosaurs. He was creative and good at drawing, sketching, taxidermy, and papier-mâché. He could make a five-foot-tall *Tyrannosaurus rex* out of strips of newspaper, glue and flour, chicken wire, and poster paint, then position the beast on a platform complete with papier-mâché flora and fauna and rocks historically accurate for the late Cretaceous period. He could create museum-quality mountings of fish, birds, and small mammals using only an epoxy compound, glass eyeballs, and his own innate understanding of sculpture, anatomy, tanning, and the natural world. Mitchell was quiet, even-tempered, and obedient. If our mother asked him to take out the garbage, for example, or feed the dogs, Mitchell didn't say just a minute. He didn't say I will soon as there's a commercial, or I did it last time, or why do I have to do everything around here. No, Mitchell got up off the couch, and he took out the trash, he fed the dogs, he did what he was told when he was told, and he did it without lip.

Every year at Halloween, Mitchell still had Easter candy. At Christmas, he had Halloween candy—even the good stuff, the miniature Hershey's and Snickers and little bags of M&M's—and when Valentine's Day rolled around, Mitchell still had a stocking full of chocolate Santas, chocolate sleighs, a Rudolph the Red-Nosed Reindeer made of chocolate.

He didn't even flaunt his stash like I would have. He didn't gloat about having it. Not unless he'd been provoked. Calling him a sissy usually worked or a pansy or a pussy or an asthmatic or some combination of these. Say something like you pussified pansy-faced sissy asthma boy! and Mitchell would open his mouth to show how slowly an agonizingly teensy sliver of a chocolate bunny's ear melts on a pink tongue. "Where's yours?" he'd say. "I'm still enjoying mine."

We each received an allowance of five bucks a week, and Mitchell, the smart child, the family genius, washed his money in the bathroom sink. He ironed it smooth. He clipped it to the clothesline that stretched across the room he shared with our brother Travis. Mitchell saved his money, Mitchell saved every last cent while I ate my Halloween candy, my Christmas candy, my Easter candy, and I spent my allowance the same day I got it, and I never, ever did anything my mother asked me to do when she asked me to do it and certainly not without questioning why I had to do it, why didn't she ask Mitchell, perfect Mitchell, her favorite, God's favorite, everyone's favorite.

Mitchell is now thirty-one years old, the director of a cardiac research lab, professionally successful, as was his destiny.

His personal life, though, in my opinion, needs work. He wants to become a father. Mitchell wants to impress his future grandchildren with his three-foot-tall jar full of quarters. But first he needs to meet a woman. He worries that if he doesn't find her, fall in love, marry, and impregnate her immediately, he'll be too old to coach his kid's soccer team.

Part of the problem is, Mitchell doesn't have much to say. This makes dating difficult.

My brother and I sometimes go for months without talking. We've gone for as long as a year without talking, not because either of us is angry with the other—repressed, unresolved childhood pain and angst aside—but because Mitchell doesn't talk. He's not chatty, not verbose, his is not a bubbly, loquacious personality. He once told me he has days where the only person he speaks to is the kid at the drive-thru window. Do you want fries with that? the kid says, and my brother tells him yes.

The last time I talked to Mitchell, it was his birthday, and our conversation went like this:

"Happy birthday, you little turd!"

"Thanks."

Silence.

"Are you still there?"

"I'm here."

Silence.

"Do you remember that time at the carnival when you puked on people?"

"Yes."

"That was hilarious!"

Nothing.

"Does your breath still smell like egg salad and feet?"

Silence.

"Do you still commit filthy and unnatural acts with barnyard animals?"

Nothing.

"I got an e-mail from this guy named Fabius Heishman. He's a representative for a pharmaceutical company. He's selling a penile enhancement product that's guaranteed. I figured you might be interested, so I forwarded it to you."

Nothing.

"Have you hung up yet?"

"I'm here."

Silence.

"Remember that time you got hit by a car?"

"Yes."

"That was hilarious!"

Nothing.

"Don't hang up."

"I won't."

We spent several more minutes in silence, and then I asked my brother did he want to hang up. He said only if you do, and I said no, I didn't want to hang up. I wanted to keep talking because even though talking to Mitchell isn't really talking, it still counts for something. We're on the same phone line at the same moment in time, we're connected.

While listening to my brother's breathing, I thought about two specific moments from our childhood. In one, I'm six years old and Mitchell is three. He's running, and just as he's about to pass me, I stick out my foot, and he's kissing the carpet and I think that's hilarious even when I'm standing with my nose in the corner, punishment for tripping my little brother, and haven't I been told?

In the other, I'm sitting on the floor on top of the register; Mitchell is sitting on my lap. We have a blanket over our heads. Whenever the furnace kicks on, hot air billows out the blanket like a parachute. I'm reading my brother a book called *Panda Cake*. "Sit still," I tell him, "and pay attention. Or I'll kick you out of my school."

I read him the story about the panda siblings whose mother gives them money to buy ingredients for her famous panda cake, but they squander it somehow, though I don't remember how, at the racetrack maybe, and it's probably the older one's idea. If they go home to their mother empty-handed, there will be hell to pay. Undoubtedly, it's the younger one who finds a way to resolve this problem, probably through his charm, good looks, ingenuity, and intelligence. I wanted to ask Mitchell if he remembered *Panda Cake*, but I was afraid to because if he didn't, I'd feel terrible. I must have read him that book at least ninety-seven times.

In my memory, I just finished reading it to him. "Now it's your turn to read," I tell him, bossy-like, and though he opens to the middle, he recites the story from the beginning, and though our mother pooh-poohs my accomplishment, saying Mitchell just has it memorized, I'm pretty sure I taught the boy to read.

"Good job, Mitchell!" I tell him, like he's a puppy I've just house-broken. "Good boy!" Then for no reason at all, I give him a hard shove and tell him he stinks, go away. I will always believe if this kid is smart, he's smart because of me. I will always be a little jealous of him, and I will always feel in charge of him, and when I grow up, a lot of guys I'll date are some girl's little brother. I'll find myself trying to bully these guys, wanting to put my foot on their throats or karate-chop them across the back. "Did you just head butt me?" one of them will say. I'll find myself trying to baby these guys, wanting to help them with their Christmas shopping, their tax returns, their home decorating.

And when my son is born, all I can see is my brother Mitchell. Those two look a lot alike. Oh, those long eyelashes wasted on a boy. Oh, that sweet smile and those pink cheeks, and what a dreamy, starry-eyed boy. Sometimes, my son is just standing there, he's gazing at the heavens, he's studying the stars, there's a beam of sunshine casting its golden light on him and him alone, and a chorus of angels sings a single holy note, and even though the boy is minding his own business, he's thinking his own thoughts, when I look at him and see my brother, I am almost overwhelmed by the urge to reach out and give that kid a hard shove. I don't, of course, but the impulse is still there.

Humping the Dinosaur

He was a red puppy with a blob of white at the tip of his tail, as if he planned to paint a portrait with ranch dressing. He had white freckles on his paws and on his chin. He had a black spot on his cheek, like a lady's beauty mark. His ears were pointy, his snout was long, his nose a good stretch from his face. He was cute, white-tipped with fuzz, pink-tongued, and he had that warm and fleeting puppy smell. He was so tiny, and he seemed so sweet and helpless and dear. I saw him in the window at the pet store, a border collie–German shepherd mix, eighty bucks, shots included. On impulse, I brought him home. I thought a pet would distract me from my problems, but instead the puppy behaved in ways that reminded me of them.

The puppy seemed neurotic. Antisocial. He seemed obsessive-compulsive. He was always scratching at himself and snarling at the other puppies in obedience school. He growled at small children. He prodded his nose toward human female crotches. He lunged at bearded men who were of above-average height.

He could be a very smelly puppy.

He reeked like something forgotten, something rotten, something feral and fecund and musky. Like rotting leaves and synthetic raccoon urine. The smell pulsated off of him when he was growling or barking or showing his teeth. He smelled bad a lot.

The puppy snarled at people on bicycles and rollerbladers and skateboarders. He didn't much care for pregnant ladies, either, like the one who strolled past our house daily. She crossed the street if she saw us on the front lawn: me trying to teach the puppy to *Sit! Stay! Be nice!* and the puppy emitting a menacing vibration from deep in his throat if he happened to see her and snapping at imaginary flies or clicking his teeth against his groin if he didn't.

I had to walk him at five in the morning so we could avoid running into other dogs. The puppy attacked other dogs. He'd fight fearlessly, though he never won, always going back for more, even after getting his ass kicked by a three-legged cocker spaniel.

But when I think back to this time, what I remember the most is the puppy humping things.

Even though I'd had him neutered, he was always humping something. The blue pillow from the couch, the couch cushions, the couch. The cloth yellow dinosaur with a voice box sewn in its belly that squealed *I'm the baby!* with each thrust. My sandal. A pile of laundry. My son's leg.

I'd hear the boy hollering for me from the living room—*Mom! Mom!*—and when I went to the living room, I'd find the boy with his hands in the air like he was showing the cops he meant no harm. The puppy's arms would be wrapped around the boy's knees; the puppy would be partying his privates against the boy's calf. *Help!* the boy would yip. *Get him off of me! Help me!* and I'd shout, *You rotten little mutt! You mangy mongrel! You nasty little cur! You bad, bad puppy!* I'd whack the puppy with a fly swatter until he let go. Or I'd use a rolled-up newspaper. Or the sandal he had recently made love to.

My son was in fifth grade when I brought home the puppy. I wanted the two of them to love each other, but it was more like jealous sibling rivalry. Sometimes, the puppy ran into the boy's room and snatched his socks or his favorite hooded sweatshirt or the really hard math homework the boy had just completed. Then the puppy ran under the dining room table to shred these things.

Other times, the puppy ran into the boy's room, jumped up on the boy's bed, and rubbed his stinky, musk-scented doggie body all over the boy's sheets. It would make the boy yell and stomp his feet and maybe even cry. *I hate that dog!* he said, while the puppy hid under the dining room table.

I too, behaved in ways that suggested I had issues. Most of my issues aren't that unusual among those of my race, class, gender, and level of education—white, middle, female, college—and these issues include low self-esteem, panic and anxiety attacks, unresolved anger toward my mother, and general bitchiness.

But my main issue was, and to some extent still is, a kind of eternal hiccup of the crowded mind. No tiny sips of water can cure it. No breathing in a paper bag can make it go away. It's what happens when I zero in on a particular thought, how I can worry that thought until I am worn out.

For example. If the cashier rings up my order, and it comes to six dollars and sixty-six cents, I will purchase a roll of Life Savers or I will put back the brick of Colby Jack, but either way, for the hours and days to come, I'll worry about what it means that *my* groceries totaled up to *that* number. Is it a sign? If so, from whom? I don't want to think about it.

Then this will happen: Because that number has appeared to me in the grocery store, I'll see it again on a license plate on the car ahead of me in traffic. It will turn out that the car just happens to be going where I'm going because they stay ahead of me for a really, really long time. This will make me nervous. The thought will occur to me that the car with that number license plate is *leading* the way. My heart will pound.

Then that number will be part of somebody's phone number, and it's imperative that I make the call. Then I'll see it on a billboard advertising sandwiches: each meatball sub is three dollars and thirty-three cents, and if you buy two, like I'd have to, well, there it is. That number will turn up when I'm playing poker, and somebody beats my pair of kings with triple sixes. A switch in my brain flicks on and off and on and off. A light in my head is flashing. A bell is ringing ding! ding! ding! I won't want to think about it, but I can't not think about it, then in the middle of the night, I will wake up to think about it some more.

I'll obsess about whether or not I turned the coffeepot off. The curling iron. The gas on the stove top. A voice in my head will say, *You better go check! You're gonna burn the house down!* I'll obsess about whether or not I locked the door. *Are you sure you locked it? Are you positive? Better go check. There could be a rapist hiding in the basement already!* I'll obsess about if that thump I heard while driving was me running over someone: an old man with a walker, a little kid on a tricycle, a bum and his GOD BLESS sign. *You better go check!*

I'll obsess about how I smell too strongly of perfume, putrid perfume, an especially loud and stinky kind I received for Mother's Day, and thus feel obligated to wear. *You reek!* the voice says. *You are offending people!* I'll obsess about whether or not the shirt I'm wearing is too tight—*You're a slut!*—and, upon deciding it is, I'll obsess about my motives for buying a too-tight shirt—*You're a slut!*—and how, maybe, in Lost and Found, there will be a sweater I can borrow. *You're a slutty slut slut,* the voice says. *And you smell like a whorehouse in France!*

And later, after I return the sweater to the cardboard Lost and Found box, I'll think I feel itchy. Like on my arms. My shoulders. My neck.

Fleas, I'll think.

Body lice.

Cooties.

The puppy did not have fleas. He had melty brown eyes the color of chocolate. He stared at me with them. He watched my every move. Sometimes, I'd glance up from the book I was reading or glance away from the movie I was watching to find the puppy staring at me, his eyes shiny and unblinking.

When he fixed those eyes on me, I did his bidding. It was like he put a hex on me, he worked his mojo. I got up at five in the morning to take him for long walks. I brushed his coat. I brushed his teeth. I ate my dinner with the puppy's head on my lap. I gave him the cheese I was about to put in my mouth and the cheese I was about to lay across my son's sandwich. In bed, I didn't dare shift my position because it might disturb him. I surrendered the softest pillow to his cause, and when I spread a blanket across the most comfortable chair, no one but the puppy sat on it ever again.

When I poured kibble—lamb meal and rice, good-quality protein, no artificial fillers—he refused to eat it unless I thumped him on his haunches and said encouraging things. *There, there! Aren't you a special man?* and *Who's a pretty baby doggie boy? Why, you are! Yes, you!* and *Eat your kibbles, honey! Yes, eat your kibbles!* Only when the puppy's confidence was up and he had been adequately praised would he eat. He'd eat, and I'd applaud—*Hooray!*—and he'd crunch his kibble and growl while wagging his tail.

The puppy didn't like to be left alone. He didn't like to be ignored. There were days when it seemed like he could never get enough attention to satisfy his need for attention. The puppy would get depressed. He'd sigh. He'd stare at the wall or at his feet in an impassive way. He'd burp like a human burps. Or he'd shred something. He'd take a book, a sweater, a twenty-dollar bill under the dining room table, and he'd shred it.

I understood him completely.

I t happens when I feel nervous or worried or anxious or angry or stressed. My thoughts get taller and heavier, stronger. They grow arms and legs. They get up, stretch, take a walk around. My thoughts bully me. *The boy was saying he had a stomachache*, they say, *and his bathroom habits seem different. It's Crohn's disease. He's going to die.*

They say, *You were moving kind of stiffly after that* Godfather Trilogy *marathon, and ever since you started drinking coffee again, you've been feeling trembly. Hate to tell ya this, but it's gotta be* Parkinson's.

They say, *That kid seems unusually tired for an eight-year-old, and his short-term memory is lousy. It is definitely chronic fatigue.*

They say, *That weird brown spot on your toe? Cancer. Of the big toe. You're going to die.*

I keep this noise in my head a secret from others. During the hours of my life away from home—when I'm at work, the grocery store, the bank, a party—there is no noise. I look and act and appear normal. I go about my day and take care of the tasks at hand. I smile. I nod. I wait my turn. I say *Yes, please!* and *Why, thank you!* and *You have a great day, too!* No one would ever know it to look at me that as soon as I'm alone I am busy busy busy in the head.

Chasing thoughts will eventually tucker a girl out. It's exhausting, and it always leads to crying. Crying because the girl thinks she's crazy, wacko, a real nutcase. Because she thinks she's alone. Because she forgot to turn on the Crock-Pot, she forgot to turn down the thermostat, she forgot to turn off the oven, so it stayed at 350 degrees all night long. She'll cry because it'll occur to her that nobody has ever loved her, nobody ever did, and nobody ever will. She'll cry because when she hugged her beloved, he tolerated her embrace, then unhooked her to ask is there any Swiss cheese in the fridge. All she wants is something that will let her hug it for as long as she wants. But she doesn't have that. So she'll cry. She'll also drink too much, smoke too much, eat too much, weigh too much, want too much. She'll worry that she's boring. She's stupid. She's needy. Instead of hiding under the dining room table to shred twenties, she'll spend them. Instead of shredding sweaters, she'll buy them. Instead of sleeping, she'll spend the night on WebMD.com, researching rare diseases she's certain will strike the people she loves. She'll cry because there's a gray hair at her temple and a weird brown spot on her big toe.

She'll also cry because, let's face it, she's a fucking mess.

When I brought home a prescription for Xanax, the people who love me cheered. "Bitch-Be-Gone pills," they said. Some of them told me to be careful because that stuff's habit-forming, while others showed up at my door, hands outstretched, saying gimme, gimme, gimme. "It's not like you had dental work done," they said. "Then you'd have Vicodin. But Xanax is good. Xanax'll do the trick. You wanna know what goes good with Xanax?" they said. "Bourbon."

Xanax does go good with bourbon, and also with Scotch. And vodka. Gin. Wine is okay, but whiskey is better. A couple Xanax, a couple shots of Maker's Mark, a few hours on the computer playing Spider Solitaire: heaven. I can gobble up a one-month supply in about a week. I had to tell my doctor you cannot give me these ever again.

I thought obedience school would do the puppy some good. I also thought the idea of it was cute. Tie a Harley-Davidson bandana around his neck. A wide orange and black Harley collar with a matching leash. A leather vest. The puppy was bad, but he was also badass.

Wanda, the dog trainer at the obedience school, said under no circumstances should one ever, ever hit a puppy. She said it's unnecessary, and there is no reason to, ever.

Instead, according to Wanda, one needs to get inside the puppy's mind. One needs to think as puppies think. One needs to psycho-analyze the puppy.

I myself had given psychoanalysis a try—twice—and I had

been kicked out of psychoanalysis—twice—so I was resistant to trying it again, though my family doctor kept enumerating the ways I might find it useful. The idea of psychoanalyzing the puppy sounded wacky to me.

Wanda was a trim, fit woman who wore her hair in a tidy gray bob. She wore high-waisted jeans and a tucked-in T-shirt that said *If only there was a man as smart as my dog!* When I told her about the yellow dinosaur and the puppy's habitual humping of it—"Like he's got a sex addiction!" I joked. "He needs a Twelve Step Program!"—she didn't laugh or even smile.

Instead, she explained some things to me. Dogs are pack animals, she said. They establish hierarchies, and if they're wired to believe they should be at the top of the hierarchy, you have to show them the error of their thinking, but you must do so in a way that's gentle and patient and loving. A neutered dog who humps is expressing his dominance, Wanda gravely informed me. Humping him expresses yours.

"So to clarify, what you're saying is that I should dry hump my dog?" I said. "I mean, I'm not misunderstanding you here, am I? I don't want to misunderstand or misinterpret or misconstrue."

Wanda was wearing sensible shoes, she had liver spots on her hands and clear blue eyes in a tanned face. She looked like a divorced high school English teacher or somebody's spinster aunt. "What you're saying is," I asked her, "if I want my dog to stop humping—which I do want, I want that very much—the only way I can make that happen is by me dry humping him. My dog."

"Yes."

That night, as my son and I were eating dinner, the puppy crawled out from under the dining room table. He had with him his friend, the yellow dinosaur. He humped it and humped it, his mouth slightly open, while the boy and I ate dinner, and we tried not to giggle, we tried not to watch, we tried to act like everyone is this crazy. This is how life is at everyone's house.

When I brought home a prescription for Paxil, the people who love me weren't surprised. "Welcome aboard!" they said. "We've been waiting for you!"

Some of them were on Paxil. Some of them took Prozac. Others took Sepram. Or Sarafem. There's Lexapro, Luvox, Lustral. There's Zoloft. It was like being in a club, it was like being in with the in crowd.

We talked about our doses. We chatted about serotonin levels. We sympathized with one another about our various side effects: nausea, drowsiness, headaches, fluctuations in weight. Those who lost weight said, *All right!* Those who gained weight said, *What the hell.* A lot of us said, *Get me to a convent, I am about as horny as a nun, alas, my private parts are of no use to me anymore.*

Paxil worked for me in that it stopped all that chaos in my head. It made my mental hiccups go away, and while I appreciated the strange silence it brought and the rest it granted, I didn't care for how Paxil pressed flat all of my feelings. It was like my mind was a chalkboard, and Paxil wiped it clean with a sponge instead of an eraser—perfectly empty, perfectly blank. It was like Paxil snipped off the tip of my tongue and all my words were blunted, no edges. When September 11 happened, I understood, intellectually, that it was sad, horrible, tragic, but I didn't feel it. I couldn't feel it. I couldn't feel anything anymore. And I knew that wasn't good.

Not long after, I didn't go to the drugstore to pick up my prescription. The drugstore called to tell me it was in, and I said I'll pick it up tomorrow. But I didn't. I didn't go to that drugstore ever again, I went off Paxil cold turkey, I haven't seen a doctor about my OCD since.

The severity of it comes and goes. It got bad when I quit smoking, it got bad when I changed jobs, it gets bad when I watch too much news. Exercise helps, though there've been a few times when it's taken three or four hours of walking to quiet my thoughts. Cutting refined sugar and processed foods out of my diet helps, and getting eight hours of sleep helps, and avoiding stress. But I don't think it's ever going to completely go away. I'm not sure I want it to. Because then who would I be? What would I think about? How would I spend my time?

I'd been napping on the couch, one of those late-afternoon naps I always regret because I wake up crabby and still tired. Even though I was groggy, even before I opened my eyes, I knew the puppy was standing there. I sensed him. He was staring at me.

He locked his gaze on mine. I saw there was a yellow dinosaur pinched between his teeth. He kept his eyes on me as he drew that thing up between his legs and humped it.

I'm the baby, I'm the baby, I'm the baby, the yellow dinosaur squeaked, and as the puppy humped it, he maintained eye contact with me. I felt like he knew my shyest secrets.

I leapt off the couch, and in a fury, I yanked it from him, and I beat him with it, and I'm embarrassed to admit what else I did.

It's not like afterward the puppy took a nap while I smoked a cigarette, though that is indeed what happened. The puppy snuck off to his hiding spot under the dining room table while I flipped through the yellow pages, chain smoking and calling strange veterinarians. I couldn't call my own. Not after what I'd done.

I finally got one on the phone who didn't act like I should be reported to the SPCA or PETA. His name was Dr. Kronkite. He said he'd talk to me for as long as I needed. He wanted to know where is the yellow dinosaur right now. He said, "Why don't I wait right here on the line while you go get it and throw it away?"

As I chatted with Dr. Kronkite, describing for him some of the puppy's behaviors, offering up my theories—separation anxiety, fear-aggression, low serotonin levels—the puppy came out from under the table. He gave me a sly look, then trotted off in the direction of the boy's bedroom.

Dr. Kronkite was saying something about doggie Prozac, its effectiveness, when I heard the puppy yelp. He came crashing out of the boy's room and went flying back under the table.

I got off the phone to get the story: The boy had caught the puppy rubbing his stinky, musky body all over the bedsheets again. But this time, the boy was prepared. He sprayed the puppy with perfume. Lots of it.

I coaxed the puppy out from under the table. "Come here, you," I said, and I held out my arms.

He sniffed my hands, whimpered, licked my fingers. The puppy army-crawled himself out from under the table and turned around twice in my lap before settling down. He smelled like decaying roses or a French whorehouse. He smelled like me. He'd eat a pound of rotten hamburger, a stick of butter, and a tampon. He'd bark at a Rottweiler, but avert his gaze from a poodle. He'd tug a pair of my dirty panties from the hamper and trot them out during a dinner party. He'd gloat about having a bone, a stick, a piece of rope, an empty Diet Dr Pepper bottle he found in the street. I'd have a doctor remove that brown spot from my big toe, I'd ask for a biopsy, I'd ask for a second opinion. I'd count to seventy-seven seven times in a row, I'd touch that spot on the back of my head where my brain is attached, I'd come home from the doctor's, the chiropractor's, the bar, and hug my dog. I was obsessed with this puppy. I still am.

Mary, Queen
of Arkansas

At age fourteen, what I wanted to be most of all was applauded, and if that wasn't possible, I wanted to be a girl in a Bruce Springsteen song. A Jersey girl. A girl named Sandy or Wendy or Candy or Cindy or Sherry, Rosalita or Crazy Janie or Mary, Queen of Arkansas. A girl idolized by an intense and poetic man who had curly dark hair and brooding dark eyes and who wore a clean white T-shirt every day. I spent hours in my bedroom, kneeling as if in supplication before my Emerson stereo fully equipped with AM/FM radio, cassette player, and turntable. I played the warped and scratchy Springsteen albums I bought at a garage sale.

Since the albums most likely to be found at a garage sale are *The Mormon Tabernacle Choir Sings Christmas Carols*; *Midnight, Moonlight & Magic: The Very Best of Henry Mancini*; and *Bagpipes of Scotland, Volume 4*, Springsteen albums are a major score even if they are, as these were, in rough shape. But I didn't care because,

to me, that made them seem more real, more true, more authentic. More like the kind of records Springsteen himself would own.
These records were naked. They weren't in sleeves, and they didn't
have covers, and the name *Jack* was written in black marker on
the red Columbia label. Jack left his albums behind because he'd
moved out in a hurry, but such haste was necessary because Jack
had been caught cheating. His wife, a woman I'd never seen before
and would never see again, told me about it. The consequence of
Jack's adultery was that his wife wrote *10 cents* on jagged pieces of
masking tape, then sold for dimes the things Jack loved best.

As I flipped through Jack's record collection, Jack's wife, a pudgy
brunette who was setting up their baby's playpen in the driveway,
called out that her soon-to-be ex just loved Springsteen, but since she
hated Springsteen almost as much as she once loved her cheater-for-a-
husband, she would let me have all five records for a quarter.

Jack's wife was gabby. She asked me how old I was, and what
grade was I in, and where did I go to school, and did I have a
boyfriend. She told me to guess how old she was. When I guessed
thirty, an answer that never failed to flatter any adult who was
being coy about age, she said not for three more weeks.

The albums included *Greetings from Asbury Park, N.J.; The
Wild, the Innocent & the E Street Shuffle; Darkness on the Edge of
Town; Born to Run;* and *Born in the U.S.A.*

Jack's wife was also selling the contents of her junk drawer, but
she hadn't bothered to dump the odds and ends in a box; she'd just
brought the junk drawer itself outside and put it on the ground next
to the mailbox and beside a wooden coat hanger. A geezer and a blue-
hair, obviously married for a hundred years or more, were rummaging
through that drawer. Otherwise, it was just me and Jack's wife.

"You're still young, so you don't know anything," Jack's wife said, plopping her fat bald baby in the playpen. "So I'm going to give you some advice. You want my advice?"

I said okay. I was sure there was nothing this lady could say that would ever have anything to do with me. Jack's wife and I had nothing in common, and I didn't see how we ever could. Love had let her down, and she'd let herself go. She had a droopy chin and a lot of black eyeliner around her eyes and she was wearing a Pittsburgh Steelers T-shirt that was much too big for her. It hung past her shorts, like a little girl wearing a nightgown except she looked too tired in the face to be a little girl. When her bald-headed baby spit out its pacifier, and the pacifier landed on the driveway, Jack's wife picked it up, popped it in her own mouth, then plugged it back in her baby's.

"Two things I want to tell you," Jack's wife said. "First of all, take your Pill. Always. Don't be sloppy! Take it at the same time every day. Don't forget to take it!" She lit a cigarette. "Second, don't get married. If you do the first, then the second should be no problem." She took my dollar, handed me my change, then asked did I know anyone who liked to read because if I did there were a whole bunch of paperback James Bond books on that table over there. "For cheap," she said.

For a girl like me—a girl growing up in a western Pennsylvania Rust Belt town; a girl whose old man goes to work clean but comes home dirty, whose mother keeps one eye on *The Young and the Restless* while folding the laundry and running the sweeper; a dreamy and moody girl, melancholy and full of angst; a girl with a talent for histrionics, sentimentality, and exaggeration, who knows in her heart she's too lyrical for the nitwits tugging at their testicles and sniffing their fingers in English class but too ornery for the mama's boys who would never dream of changing their own spark plugs, not that they'd even have at hand the tools necessary for performing such a task, not that they'd even know how to change their own spark plugs let alone their oil or their brakes—a honey-tongued, blue-collar bastard like Bruce Springsteen is hard to resist. At age thirty-two, I would proclaim that it'd take a whole lot more than pretty words to make me lay down, but when I was fourteen years old and kneeling as if in supplication before my Emerson stereo, I listened to Springsteen in the privacy of my bedroom, the curtains drawn, the shades down, my heart pounding. Behind a door that was closed, then locked, Bruce Frederick Joseph Springsteen demanded to know if love is wild and if love is real. He was pleading to give him one last chance to make it real. He was promising to liberate me, to confiscate me, he said, "I want to be your man," and even if I wasn't perfect, I wasn't a beauty, I didn't need to feel bad about it because in his eyes, hey, I was all right. He accepted me just the way I am. Springsteen swore he loved his girl so much that he wanted to die with her on the streets tonight in an everlasting kiss. There was something dynamic and sexy, beautiful and brave, about such a man. I wanted to marry him or someone exactly like him. At age fourteen, I wrote down the things Springsteen said in my diary, then I lifted the needle so I could hear him say them again.

By age thirty-two, I had some things in common with Jack's ex-wife: motherhood, divorce, part-time income generated from garage sales. What happened to the girl I used to be?

Love had let that girl down. She'd been sloppy about taking her Pill, which meant she ended up married, then divorced. She didn't believe in Springsteen anymore. In fact, she thought Bruce Springsteen was full of shit. For many years, she could only listen to him if she was drunk.

The girl and I both knew this was pathetic. So did our friends who would agree to come to a party at my house only on the condition that the girl I used to be didn't get drunk and weepy and play Springsteen, but if she did, she didn't dance that hump-the-wall dance she always dances to Springsteen, but if she had to, she didn't, under any circumstances, sing along with Springsteen.

"Especially 'Rosalita,' " the man in my life said.

Al is usually indifferent to Bruce Springsteen, though there have been times when he's allowed me to put *Born to Run* on the turntable, and he's sat patiently while I insisted he listen to the words, man, just listen to the words. "I like him okay," Al said, "and other people might like him, too, if you weren't always trying to cram him down our throats." Like Springsteen was a horse pill or my boss's homely daughter that I was trying to find a date to the senior prom.

"That dance you did to 'Rosalita' last Thanksgiving?" Al said. "When you humped the wall? I thought it was kind of cool, but I think it made some people feel uncomfortable. I'm pretty sure that's when people started putting on their coats. And your singing? Well, I thought your singing was awesome, just hilarious, but that's just me."

I told Al that he wasn't exactly someone who'd be mistaken for Bruce Springsteen, either. But I shouldn't have been insulted. Because it's true: I'm a terrible dancer, awkward and noodle-armed, lascivious and likely to stumble, to trip, to fall down, and I'm a horrible singer, warbly and wobbly and quivering, breathy and giggly and off-key. My performances don't bring anything positive to anyone's Springsteen experience, except maybe alcohol and enthusiasm.

"I am so much cooler than Mr. B.S.," Al said, "you just don't know it yet."

What then occurred to me was this: maybe I couldn't be a girl in a Springsteen song, maybe I'd never be loved by an intense and poetic man, but I could be the mother of a Springsteen. I could live with that. I could live through it. At age thirty-two, I decided what I wanted most of all was to be the mother of a guitar-playing boy.

Bruce Springsteen's mother may have taken out a loan to buy her son his first guitar, but I would do my son even better, I would use my MasterCard to buy him one. It wasn't cheap, but the kid at the music store said it was called a Baby Taylor, and he seemed excited that a mother would purchase such an instrument for her ten-year-old. This kid was pierce-lipped and unnaturally pale, he'd painted his fingernails black, but his approval convinced me I had done right by my boy.

In my daydreams, a guitar son would be the most fun kind of son to have, not so oafish and hungry like a football son, not so in need of money for computer chips and space camp like a brainiac son. Besides, sports and nerd things are boring, while rock and roll, as a guitar boy could provide, is cool. He would rev his motorcycle in front of my house, guitar strapped to his back, and tucked away in his back pocket, he'd keep a notebook in which he scrawled poems about the beauty of a mother's love that he would later turn into songs about the beauty of a mother's love. His hair would be moppy and his face would be unshaven, but this would not detract from his moody-but-vulnerable handsomeness. He'd wear a white T-shirt every day.

One day, my guitar son would come to me, he would tell me this is his one last chance to make it real, he's moving to New York or to Los Angeles or to whatever American city is most important to the music scene at that time, and he'd express his gratitude for all the support and encouragement I'd given him over the years. "It's really meant a lot," he'd say, and that's when I'd tell him I have a little something for you. I'd hand him the big pile of cash I'd been setting aside for years and years, money I'd scrimped and sacrificed to save so he could follow his heart, chase his dream, know his destiny.

Furthermore, I believed starting my son with guitar lessons now, at age ten, would make him popular with girls once he got to high school, and I knew it would win him the favor of people sitting around the fire on camping trips.

"I hate to butt in," Al said, "but maybe you should ask him if he wants to take guitar lessons. It wouldn't hurt to have his input."

I asked the boy did he want to take guitar lessons.

He said no.

"This is just a suggestion," Al said. "You can take it or leave it. It's just a crazy idea I had. But I was thinking. Since you're so interested in the guitar, maybe you should learn to play it. Maybe it's you who should sign up for lessons. What about that?"

The idea was absurd. I had no interest in learning how to play the guitar. I looked at Al and raised just one eyebrow. Earlier he had been teaching the boy to speak in a British accent by shouting the words *I want a baked potato!* Their accents were terrible.

Then the two of them shouted, *Tirty-tree and a turd, farty-far and a fart*. It was, Al explained, a lesson in fractions recited in an Irish accent. I didn't think this man should have any say in my son's musical education.

When I asked the boy why not, why didn't he want to take guitar lessons, he said because he didn't feel like it.

"You don't feel like it!" I said. "Well," I told him. "You have a choice. You can take guitar lessons or you can fold a basket of laundry that contains my bras and panties. It's entirely up to you. You decide which you feel like doing, then come tell me your decision."

The guitar teacher had two things in common with Bruce Springsteen: strumming and plucking a stringed instrument, and the same initials. The guitar teacher's name was Bill Schatz. I found Mr. Schatz in the phone book under the listing for the Western Colorado Academy of Music, which was really just a cramped one-room storefront downtown next door to the Christian Science Reading Room. I signed the boy up to take guitar lessons from Mr. Schatz every Tuesday night from six-thirty to seven-fifteen.

Mr. Schatz was sixty-eight years old. He had thin white hair that he combed down flat so it spread like wispy fingers over his forehead. His face was round, his glasses were round, his shoulders were round, his gut was round. He was a stocky, bulky guy. When the weather was above sixty degrees, Mr. Schatz wore a short-sleeved, loudly patterned Hawaiian shirt. When temperatures dropped below sixty, he wore an acrylic powder-blue sweater with a snowflake pattern across the chest. The sweater was tight, accentuating his pregnant ladyesque belly. He wore black jeans and cheap white tennis shoes. He was sick a lot, frequently blowing his nose into a white hanky.

"What do you think of your guitar teacher?" I asked my son. "What do you think of Mr. Schatz?"

The boy said Mr. Schatz was weird. He commented on how Mr. Schatz kept asking us to repeat ourselves. We couldn't tell whether this was because Mr. Schatz was hard of hearing or because the things we said were unfathomable. "What?!" he'd say, scrunching up his face, and "Huh?!"

I thought this made the guy almost impossible to have a normal conversation with, but Al, who is slightly hard of hearing himself, believed otherwise.

"Mr. Schatz is a genius!" Al explained. "He communicates through music! The man's head is just so full of music that there's not room for anything else." If Al could pick any talent for himself, it would be a talent for music. When Al was a boy in Detroit, he'd taken accordion lessons, but when his father got laid off, the family couldn't afford the lessons, and that was the end of Al's musical training. One was supposed to see this as tragic. One was not supposed to picture Al, clad in lederhosen, a crown of edelweiss on his head, playing polkas in a beer tent. One was not supposed to think maybe his old man's getting the ax was a blessing in disguise, and if one did think this, one was not supposed to say so.

Mr. Schatz didn't play polkas. He was a jazz guitarist, light jazz, the kind of music you would never associate with smoky nightclubs and turtleneck-wearing, finger-snapping cool cats who inject heroin and wear berets. No, this was the sort of jazz you might pound the phone against your head in time to as you wait for the next available customer service representative to take your call. Mr. Schatz was good at playing this so-called mellow jazz, and had, in fact, played with Henry Mancini at Red Rocks Amphitheater. He'd been invited to go on the road with Mancini's band, but because he married Mrs. Schatz, the girl of his dreams, Mr. Schatz gave up the road and became a middle school band director. Mr. Schatz and his wife, Dorothy, raised two boys, one of whom provided Mr. Schatz with a grandson named Hans, while the other provided a grandson named Luke and a granddaughter named Leia. Mr. Schatz showed us a picture of his grandchildren, little moppets with blond pageboy haircuts. All three looked exactly alike.

"Hans and Luke and Leia," I said. "Your sons must've really liked *Star Wars*."

"What!?" Mr. Schatz said.

"Your grandchildren are named Hans and Luke and Leia like the characters in *Star Wars*?"

"Oh," he said. "Yes."

Even at age ten, my son knew Mr. Schatz was uncool.

But Al took one look at Mr. Schatz's guitar, a Gibson L-5 the man bought a million years ago when he was seventeen. It was an ornate piece of wood, stunningly beautiful, Al thought. The blond maple, the hand-polished frets, hand-polished neck and body, oiled fingerboard and bridge. Yes, Al thought, it's an instrument that's lovely to look at, but it's also beautiful to listen to, like a thousand angels singing a thousand truths about one's innate goodness—and Al was overcome by what is commonly known among music store owners as "guitar lust." Before long, Al would buy one guitar, and then another, and then another. He would spend thousands of dollars on guitars and guitar accessories. Strings, a tuner, stands, picks and straps, a polishing cloth, hard cases. But to justify putting guitars and guitar accessories on his Discover card, Al decided he needed to learn how to play the guitar.

He, too, signed up for lessons with Mr. Schatz.

"What kind of music do you fellows like?" Mr. Schatz asked during their first lesson.

Al gushed that he loved music, that he had an appreciation for all different kinds of music, that music made him feel good, and it made him feel happy and alive, and that he was excited about learning how to read music, how to play music, especially the guitar.

The boy said he didn't know.

"Sure you do, son!" I said. I was sitting in the corner. I'd brought along my checkbook to balance so I could fake busyness but still witness the boy's musical awakening. "He likes Bruce Springsteen!" I told Mr. Schatz.

"What?!" the old man said.

"Springsteen!"

Mr. Schatz said, "Oh."

I didn't know whether Mr. Schatz thought I was inaudible or idiotic, but in either case, he was moving on. He told the boy and Al to open their *Mel Bay's Modern Guitar Method, Grade 1* to page one, and their first lesson began.

These lessons would be a terrible thing to sit through, though, as week after week, month after month, it became obvious that my son was not lying when he said he didn't feel like learning to play the guitar. He had no interest in starring as the guitar son of my dreams. Not even when I told him I'd give him some money to move to L.A. The boy liked knowing how to pluck the notes to

"Shave and a Haircut, Two Bits" but otherwise showed no inclination toward learning how to play the guitar.

In fact, he seemed to be in deep denial that he was even taking guitar lessons. As Mr. Schatz explained something—which frets to hold down with which fingers to play a C, for example, or how to keep time—the boy would tug his new Homie out of his pocket and he'd hold it out for inspection, saying, "See what I have?"

"What?!" Mr. Schatz said.

"See my Homie?"

Homies were small plastic figurines depicting Mexican-American characters with names like Bobby Loco, Mariachi Pedro, Bubbles, and La Chunky. Homies could be purchased for fifty cents from vending machines located in grocery stores and Mexican restaurants. My son was building his Homies a barrio out of Legos, a structure he called "Ashbury Park." I was never convinced Homies were good toys because they hurt terribly when you stepped on them with bare feet, but I agreed to buy the boy ten every time he practiced for half an hour. In a few weeks' time, he accumulated a hundred, and since he didn't need or want any more, he quit practicing altogether.

But the guitar lessons were the high point of Al's Tuesdays, something he looked forward to all week. Mr. Schatz taught Al how to play Spanish ditties like "Malagueña" and "Caliente" and English-speaking classics like "Georgia" and "The Girl from Ipanema." Al would practice and practice these songs at home, but when he played for Mr. Schatz, it was like he'd never practiced at all. "I don't understand," he said apologetically. "I worked on this all week."

"What?!" said Mr. Schatz.

"I guess I just need to prac—"

"You just need to practice more," Mr. Schatz interrupted. "Both of you. Especially since your recital is coming up next month. You want to sound good at the recital, don't you?"

My son said he didn't want to be in any recital.

I, however, loved the idea. It seemed to me that once the boy stood in front of an audience, once he'd heard his name spoken over loudspeakers, once he'd taken a bow, then stood graciously for a moment to receive his due applause that would more than likely erupt into a standing ovation, he might come around to this music thing. It might be something he mentioned during the little speech he'd give when he went onstage to receive his Grammy. "I thank God my mother made me play in that recital," he'd say, and, "I thank God for my mother."

"We can't wait for the recital!" I said.

Al mumbled something about how he didn't want to be in any recital, either, and for once Mr. Schatz not only heard what some-one said, he seemed to comprehend it. "Well, I understand you feel nervous, Allen," he said. "Stage fright is very real, and it happens to us all. But if you practice a lot, you can overcome stage fright." Mr. Schatz's voice had taken on a bossy, bullying tone that proba-bly put any number of seventh- and eighth-grade trombone players back in line and kept the flutists on edge. When Al mumbled that he really, really, really didn't want to be in the recital, Mr. Schatz said nonsense. It would require a true commitment to practice, but with hard work and a little bit of confidence, he'd do fine.

The piece Mr. Schatz assigned Al to perform was called "Far-ruca." A form of Flamenco music, farruca is said to be "the most Gypsy of all the Spanish dances." Upon playing the last note,

Mr. Schatz wanted Al to shout "Farruca!" in a bold and impassionate voice, and every time Al did, I pictured him in black breeches and boots, the flouncy white blouse, a long black vest trimmed with gold braiding, the red sash around his waist, and the gold hoop in his ear. He practiced that two-minute song, over and over, faster and faster, again and again; he played "Farruca" so much that it became the sound track of our lives, the music I heard in my head while I walked the dog, stirred the sauce, tried to read. The boy hummed it while playing with his Legos. Al whistled it, tapped it, played it on an air guitar while waiting for the pasta to boil. "Farruca" became the sound track to our dreams.

"Farruca!" Al shouted, then caught me smirking at him. "What?" he said. The guitar was sitting on his lap like a sexy girl, and Al was hugging it from behind, his hands on its hips. "If you don't mind," he said, peering at me from around the guitar's curvy waist, "I need to practice. I have a recital coming up."

The recital took place on a Sunday afternoon. It was held in the music hall at the local college. Parents and grandparents, brothers and sisters, aunts and uncles, shifted in their seats, straining their necks to catch a glimpse of the kid that was theirs. We all clapped politely as the student musicians from the Western Colorado Academy of Music traipsed across the stage—nineteen ten-year-olds and one fifty-three-year-old man—carrying violins, guitars, flutes, trumpets, piano music. My son was the boy with one hand in his pocket and a guitar strapped to his back; Al was the nervous guy, pale and sweaty and wearing a white T-shirt and black sweater vest.

The boy played "Ode to Joy" perfectly, though without emotion, a lackluster performance. Afterward, as the audience applauded, instead of taking a bow, the boy rolled his eyes and nodded impatiently, like an underling was telling him something he already knew.

Al bombed his performance. From the first awkward note he played, I knew it would be bad. It got worse. His timing was off, he missed notes, what should have sounded smooth and melodic sounded chaotic and irregular and traumatized. The two minutes went by very, very slowly. My son, sitting beside me, shook his head. "Oh, Al," the boy said in what was probably his first moment of true empathy. "Oh, Al," I agreed. It was a terrible thing to watch. At the end of the song, there was silence. Then Al shouted "Farruca!" in a bold and impassioned voice. It was an act of bravery and courage.

While Al took his bow, as he'd been instructed to do, the audience, made up mostly of parents, siblings, and grandparents, applauded politely.

Then Mr. Schatz, who'd been sitting in the front row, stood up. Mr. Schatz faced the audience. Mr. Schatz projected his voice so everyone could hear him, even the people in the balcony, even the people in the very last row. "Didn't Allen try hard!" Mr. Schatz said. "Allen gets a little nervous, but he still tried his very best! Let's give him another round of applause!"

My ex-husband didn't have any record albums, he didn't buy CDs. I don't know if he's ever been to any concerts. In the car, while he was driving, he'd turn on the radio, sometimes a country music station, sometimes a conservative talk show, but it was more like background noise. Music didn't seem to be part of him. I have no idea what songs correspond with what moments of his life. That I was once married to a man who didn't dance, who didn't sing, who listened to music without really hearing music, seemed remarkable to me. I wouldn't make that mistake again.

As Mr. Schatz led the audience in another round of applause, as the audience clapped and Al turned red and bowed before slinking offstage, as the boy tugged on my sleeve asking can we go to Dairy Queen, I overheard what the old lady sitting in the row ahead of me said. She leaned toward her middle-aged daughter and spoke loudly. She said, "Well, isn't that nice! How they let that mentally retarded fella out to be in the recital just like everyone else! Those mentally retarded sure have come a long way!"

I was just about to lean forward and tap her hand, and tell her *Lady, I am going to marry that retard someday,* when Al appeared, guitar in hand. He was motioning for me to come on, come on. He was tilting his head frantically toward the exit. Al was whispering, "Let's go, let's go, let's go." In the car, he said there were two things he wanted to say: Yes, we were most definitely going to Dairy Queen; and no, we were not listening to Springsteen, so don't ask.

The Boy, Again

Yesterday the boy didn't get out of bed until two-seventeen in the afternoon. I was sitting on the coffee table, watching *Guiding Light* and telling myself during the commercial break that if there wasn't anything good on VH1 or E! Entertainment Television, or if both of those channels were also on commercial, I would take it as a sign that I had to eat another Oreo cookie. But before I could find out how TV would once again direct my behavior, the boy came moping down the stairs, his hair hanging in his eyes, his gray T-shirt and denim cargo shorts the same gray T-shirt and denim cargo shorts he's worn every day since the last day of school. His posture was hunched, slouchy, drooping. His breath was putrid. He smelled unfresh, he looked unwashed. He said he'd slept so late because he'd stayed up playing Halo until four o'clock this morning, and would I please make him two grilled cheese sandwiches with extra cheese and could Louis sleep over tonight?

I said no.

He said why.

It used to be he didn't ask me why because we both already knew the answer. But I always enjoyed reminding him. I savored any opportunity that allowed me to point out I'm bigger than you, I'm stronger than you, I'm smarter than you, and I make more money, therefore, my wish is your command. There was a time when we both liked hearing me say this. I liked it because of the power that comes from oppressing a small child. It's a rush.

The boy liked it because I told him he did. I told him there is no denying I am all of those things. I am also capable and confident and competent, calm and committed to raising him up right.

"Why can't Louis sleep over?" he said.

"Because."

"Why because?"

But now that the boy is thirteen years old, he doesn't necessarily buy that I am capable, confident, competent, calm, or committed. He's witnessed too much of my bungling tomfoolery, my disinterest and neurosis, my negligence in fulfilling my responsibilities to him, my son, the only child I will ever have. On occasion, when I'm feeling guilty or insecure about how I've been treating him, when I'm worrying about whether or not I've been good enough and I'm suspecting that I haven't been, I'll ask him how am I doing, am I doing all right, is there anything you need that I'm not doing?

He always reassures me. He always says everything is fine. You're doing good, he says. You're a good mother.

You need anything, kid, you just let me know.

I will, he says, and in that moment, I'll give him a cookie or a hug or I'll say go get my purse so I can give you some money. I adore you, here's five dollars.

But in this moment, I was finding him very irritating. Because he was asking me yet again.

"Why can't Louis sleep over?"

"Because."

It was nothing personal against Louis, who seems like a nice enough kid, though once when he slept over, Louis ate three double-cheese grilled cheese sandwiches, then half an hour later, turned pale and clammy, sweaty and gut-rumbling. Around our house, Louis is known as The Shrieker because he occasionally releases strange, high-pitched, excited-sounding shrieks. *Eeep! Eeep! Eeep!* The first time he slept over, I shot up from a dead sleep to his racket, my heart pounding, wondering what the hell was that.

But you can't say anything about how weird Louis is in front of the boy. Because if you do, he'll turn self-righteous and P.C., he'll scold you for your insensitivity. He'll say, "I would really appreciate it if you didn't refer to my friend as 'The Shrieker.' His name is Louis, and he has Tourette's syndrome. He's also lactose intolerant. Your making fun of him just adds to the problem of hate in this world."

But neither dairy products nor neurological diseases were the reason Louis couldn't sleep over, nor was it because he'd be a bother. All he'd do is sit up in the boy's room, eating cheese-free pizza and Oreos, drinking cans of Red Bull, shrieking, and playing Halo on the boy's Xbox 360. The two of them would stay up all night.

It's that it was my thirty-fifth birthday. Al walked to Cub Foods and came back with a dozen roses. My mother sent two ten-dollar bills in a card. The boy gave me presents: A tin of Last Supper

After Dinner Mints. A rubber pretzel. A silver ring. A Hopalong Cassidy shot glass.

"Do you like your presents?" the boy asked.

I said yes. To prove I meant it, I gave him one of the tens.

He seemed pleased. He said he thought I'd like that stuff. "Let me know when you're going to use that shot glass," he said. "I want to be there when you do."

Then he said, "So why can't Louis come over?"

Then I said, "Boy, what the hell do you want from me? Are you purposely trying to make me crazy?"

Then the boy revealed that he's clever when he wants to be. Instead of asking why Louis couldn't sleep over at our house, he asked if he could sleep over at Louis's. My policy on the boy wanting to go to someone else's house has always been yes. Of course. Absolutely. Bye-bye, boy! Have fun!

"Happy birthday, Mom," he said as he was walking out the door. "Enjoy that shot glass!"

The boy is now five feet, four inches tall and weighs one hundred ten pounds. Heightwise, he's bigger than me and he's probably stronger, but he's not heavier. My extra weight plus the element of surprise means I can wrestle him to the floor every time. He's got an application in at Cub Foods for the position of stock boy. Until that comes through, he's broke. But he's resourceful: in a pinch and desperate for cash, the boy takes a few video games, CDs, or DVDs to the pawnshop.

The boy and I have different opinions about which one of us is smarter.

His dietary habits are disgusting. He eats grilled cheese, pepperoni pizza with extra cheese, and Oreo cookies crushed over chocolate ice cream. His skin is clear, his hair is shiny, his eyes are bright. Something he does in the bathroom causes the toilet to clog. This happens so often that he made a sign to warn the next sitter that there's a problem. DO NOT FLUSH, it says. DO NOT POOP.

Except for the time and energy devoted to mirror gazing and smoothing down his hair—he has some unfortunate cowlicks—the boy's personal hygiene is tragic. His room smells like boy, which means it smells hormonal. Like burnt metal and overripe fruit, like sweaty socks and Axe body spray. If he is not told to change his sheets, the boy will not change his sheets. If he is not reminded to brush his teeth, he will not brush his teeth. If he is not shamed into showering, he wouldn't think of showering. It takes telling him he stinks, or that he looks grubby, or saying what are you, a Frenchman?

He'll say you're not nice, you're mean, are you xenophobic, but he'll take a shower. He'll be in there for weird amounts of time: either less than two minutes or more than forty-five.

My life was easier when he was little. I liked him best when he was five months old. Before he had speech and mobility. Before he had opinions of his own and beliefs that weren't mine. I could spread a blanket across the living room floor and put him on it and that's where he stayed until I picked him up and put him somewhere else.

These days, some of my biggest concerns are with his politics, his vision for the future, who or what he is versus who or what he might become. Sometimes I wonder about him. Some of the things that come out of his mouth give me pause.

The boy says he opposes gun control, for example. Considering his DNA—a father who belongs to the NRA, a grandfather who had me and my prom date pose for pictures in front of the living room gun cabinet—there's no doubt about it: a mixture of potassium nitrate, charcoal, and sulfur runs through the boy's veins. It's why he believes there should be a law requiring everyone to be armed at all times, even little kids.

"Especially little kids," he said, "because what if someone tries to kidnap you when you're walking to school. What do you do then?"

"Well," I said, "you employ the techniques you learned regarding Stranger Danger. You shout 'No!' and 'I don't know you!' and 'You're not my daddy!' while you run away. That's what you do."

"Uh, Mr. Stranger?" he said, sounding creepily like Scarlett O'Hara or Blanche DuBois. "Uh, excuse me, Mr. Stranger, sir, but you are not my daddy? I don't know you? Please don't touch my private parts, Mr. Stranger, because if you do I will have to shout 'No'?"

Then he pointed his finger like a gun at some invisible Mr. Stranger's private parts, squinted one eye, clicked the trigger, blew on it.

"What was that?" I asked him, and "Who are you?"

He said he was a concerned citizen.

Another time he told me he doesn't like skateboarders because they smoke weed. White people who have dreadlocks are on his list of people he doesn't like because, he said, they smoke ganja. He said there is only one way to explain people who dress like vampires and those freaky people from the Society for Creative Anachronism who wear capes and swordfight in the park: they've been smoking reefer.

But he reserves his deepest animosity for hippies.

"Hippies?" I asked. "How can you hate hippies? Hippies are harmless. That's how we know they're hippies. What's a hippie ever done to you?"

He raised his eyebrows. He snorted. He asked did I think smoking dope was harmless?

I thought it would be best if I kept my mouth shut.

"Have you ever heard of a little thing called 'Marijuana is a gateway drug'?" he said. He said hippies are high on dope, they're wasted out of their gourd, and it's why they're hula hooping and listening to Pink Floyd and the Grateful Dead all the time. He said hippies need to know the answer is soap, not dope. He was smirking, his tone was smug, self-satisfied.

When I wondered out loud if it was hypocritical for a boy with hygiene such as his to even have an opinion about the bathing habits of hippies, he asked did I want him to be a doper, and jeez, he showers when he's dirty, which is why he doesn't go outside, so he doesn't get dirty, and besides, what about global warming? Shouldn't we be trying to conserve our freshwater resources?

Then there's the day the boy arrived home from school and immediately wanted to know would I make him a grilled cheese sandwich. When I asked how was your day, he revealed his plan to live in a house that has a hot tub, central air, and wall-to-wall carpeting. He said he hated National Public Radio and its supporters, and when he got his license, there would be no more NPR in the car.

He talked and talked. He said he hated Bob Dylan, Bruce Springsteen, Jim Morrison, and Kurt Cobain, but he loved cash money, Donald Trump, high-stakes poker, and the gigantic tub of cheese curls you can only buy at Sam's Club. He said someday he was going to have a Lamborghini, he was going to have a Viper, he was going to have a Jaguar, he was going to have a Porsche, could he have another grilled cheese sandwich? He talked so much, so fast, and he seemed so chatty and hungry, that I thought maybe he'd encountered some hippies on the way home, maybe they held him down and blew pot smoke in his face, maybe the boy was stoned.

He wasn't. It had been Career Day at school, and that's what got him riled up: the future. His future. He was excited about his future. After listening to some of the speakers—an investment banker; a certified public accountant; Jacob's dad, who owns a Saturn dealership—he decided that when he goes to college he will major in business, he will specialize in purchasing and acquisitions, he will make a buttload of money, and it was all I could do to keep from putting down my foot and dashing his dreams and telling him over my dead body you're going into purchasing and acquisitions.

"You're just a child," I said. "How do you even know about purchasing and acquisitions? Who have you been talking to?"

I thought maybe he'd been talking to his grandfather, that my father had gotten to him somehow. Or else Nancy Reagan and that this-is-your-brain-on-drugs public service announcement. Or my brother the cop. Or that maybe the boy had fallen asleep with Fox Television on in the background, and while he was sleeping, certain unpleasant ideologies threw down anchor in his subconscious.

"So does this mean you're a Republican?" I said. "Over my dead body. Not as long as you live in my house."

The boy wondered out loud if it was hypocritical when a Democrat makes her son into a political prisoner. "You're mean," he said.

"And another thing," I told him. "I won't pay for you to be a business major. Not one dime."

The boy said he was going to report me to Amnesty International.

After another late night of Halo at Louis's house, the boy came home shortly after two o'clock this afternoon. He seemed agitated, excited, distressed. He was out of breath and bare-foot. There was a long scratch on his face, and there were smaller ones on his arms and legs and ankles. "Where are your shoes?" I asked him. "What happened to you?"

He held up his sock. He pointed at a small dark spot. "That's blood," he told me. "*Blood.*"

"What happened?" I asked again.

"The cat," he said. "Louis's cat."

Only half an hour before, Louis was still asleep, but the boy was awake, and he was bored, and he didn't know where Louis's mom was, so he figured he'd get his stuff together and walk home. He was in the process of packing up his Xbox 360 when Louis's cat came flying out of nowhere. Louis's cat landed on him, hooked its claws into him, his arm, his leg, his foot, his face. The claws were like razors. Louis's cat hissed and snarled, and after the boy wres-tled it off of him, he flung it across the room. He ran but he went the wrong way, he couldn't find the door to get out of the house. Louis's cat was chasing him, and it got him, it backed him into a corner, hissing all the while in a very intimidating and upsetting way. The boy didn't know what to do. He yelled for Louis, but that guy can sleep through anything, and he didn't want to kick

Louis's cat because it was little, and it's a cute little cat when it's not attacking people, and besides, kicking it would be cruelty to animals, and he'd already thrown it across the room once, which he felt really bad about. The boy hates when people are cruel to animals.

"What did you do?" I asked.

"I didn't know what to do," he said.

That's when Louis's other cat pounced on Louis's vicious cat. Both cats were howling and snarling and hissing, and Louis even slept through that racket. But the boy recognized this as his one chance to escape, and he took it. He fled out the back door and didn't stop running until he got home.

"My shoes are back at Louis's house," the boy was saying. "I left my Xbox 360 back there, too." He was still a little breathless. "What?" he said. "What? Why are you looking at me and smiling? Don't look at me."

I denied that I was looking at him.

"Stop looking at me!" he said. "Why are you looking at me and laughing?"

"I'm not laughing!"

"You're laughing at me!" he shouted.

The boy stomped off to his room, he slammed the door, and normally, I wouldn't put up with the shouting, the stomping, or the slamming. But I felt bad. Because I had been smiling, and I did laugh, and I know that an unempathetic mother has been the downfall of many a man who might have otherwise been great. I knocked on his door and told him I really love that Hopalong Cassidy shot glass he gave me. Did he want to see me do a shot?

He said no.

I felt even worse.

My thirteen years of parenting this boy can be summed up in three sentiments:

I adore you.

What the hell do you want from me now?

I'm sorry! I'm sorry! I'm sorry!

I'm sorry, I could tell him. I'm sorry I laughed at you, and I'm sorry you don't live in the house where all the kids in the block like to hang out. I'm just not that kind of mother, and usually, I'm not sorry about it, but sometimes I am. I'm sorry I didn't serve you a wider variety of foods, because if I had maybe you'd eat something other than grilled cheese and pizza. But I'm especially sorry about the summer of 1996. Sometimes I wonder if that's where things went wrong.

That summer I was pretty depressed. My marriage to the boy's father was scabby and scaly and covered with warts; I was broke and unemployed and unhappily living in a state that bordered Utah. Getting out of bed and staying out was an achievement that warranted Oreo cookies. But there came a time when Oreo cookies were no longer an incentive. I was twenty-five years old; the boy was four.

Each morning when I got up, I poured the boy a bowl of Cheerios and a glass of milk, and I turned on his cartoons for him to watch. Then I went back to bed so I could wallow in my misery in comfort. At noon, I got up, fixed the boy a turkey sandwich and another glass of milk, and because I knew I really needed to spend some quality time with my son, I watched his cartoons with him until I dozed off on the couch. At four o'clock, I woke up for *The Oprah Winfrey Show*; at five, I heated up some fish sticks for dinner. If he'd been good, I allowed the boy to drink one can of Pepsi. After seven, when long-distance rates were cheaper, I called everyone I knew who might be sympathetic to my misery. It was not a long list.

Over time, however, as that list grew even shorter, I started spending more and more time in AOL chat rooms. Those chat rooms must've cost fifty bucks a minute because they added thousands of dollars to my Discover card bill. I once found myself in one chat room where, weirdly enough, all the men were named Dom, every single one of them. Dom Jacob. Dom Wilson. Dom Tyrel. Having grown up around a lot of Italians, I understood "Dom" was short for "Dominick," and when I tried to initiate chat room conversations with these many Doms, they seemed irritated.

You're a pushy little wench, one Dom typed. *I think you need a spanking.*

Another Dom told me to shut up, he didn't give me permission to speak, and when I said look, buddy, *I* don't remember giving *you* permission to speak, either, so why don't *you* shut up, he said I didn't have the personality of a submissive, he was reporting me to the moderator, and I was banned from the Story of O chat room forever.

One morning, after I'd been up all night in a chat room devoted to people who were professional vampires—*What do you mean, "professional"*? I kept asking. *Do you mean I could hire you to bite someone's neck? Do you charge extra to break the skin?*—I rose from bed to pour the boy's Cheerios. Maybe I was still half asleep—I couldn't have been awake, at least not entirely—because I saw the boy standing in front of the television, sucking his thumb and staring up at a face on the screen. The face was a blue rectangle, with black dots for eyes, and a black line for a mouth. It took up the entire TV screen. The face was talking to my son, its mouth opening and closing, its black dot eyes blinking. *Tell her you need to go outside and play*, the Television Face was saying. *Tell her to take you outside to play*.

It's embarrassing that my vision was not God or an angel or a saint, it wasn't even brought on by magic mushrooms or serious psychosis. It was my own guilty conscience delivering me a life lesson through the medium I understood the best: TV. I obeyed the message I received from the Television Face. "Get your shoes on," I told the boy. "I am taking you to the park."

You'd think he would have been happy, but the boy didn't seem happy.

It was too hot to go outside, he said. It was too hot to walk. He didn't like going to the park. He didn't want to go. He wanted to stay home. He wanted to watch cartoons.

I knew what he meant. I don't like to go outside, either. I have never seen a reason to go outside unless it's to get in a car that will take me to another place to go inside. When I was a child, my mother swept me outside with her broom. Out, out! she'd say, and I'd go outside, I'd go outside and sit on the front steps, waiting to be let back inside.

"You're going," I told the boy. "The Television Face told Mommy to take you outside, so you are going outside! You're going to do all the things normal children your age do! So get your butt on that swing and start swinging! Now!"

Years later, the boy still resists going outside. He says he doesn't like the sun. He says it smells funny outside. If you tell him that funny smell is the smell of the outdoors, clean air, he'll say it makes him sneeze, it gives him a headache, and if he needed to smell the outdoors, he'd take a whiff of Fresh Scent Tide.

At nine o'clock p.m., the boy emerged from his room. He'd washed the blood off his arms and leg and he seemed to be in a better mood. He announced he was starving, he asked if I would fix him two grilled cheese sandwiches, he said he and Louis had been IM'ing.

He wanted to know if Louis could sleep over tonight.

Is this boy for real? Is he normal? Does he have the skills he needs to survive? He's so different from me. When I was his age, small children were left in my care, and I rooted through their mother's medicine cabinets in search of a small white pill called Valium. Because I didn't like to be in my room, I popped out the window screen and climbed out. I smoked pot with the high school senior across the street. But I also combed my hair and wore clean underwear and took some pride in my appearance.

It seems to me that any human boy who will be old enough to vote in less time than it would take for me to pay off a new car should know to brush his teeth every day without my having to tell him to. The boy should know to go outside into the bright sun-shiny daytime, he should want to go outside, he shouldn't want to be so pale. He should prefer interacting with others to endless hours of slack-jawed, mouth-breathing video-game playing, and he should, over the course of a summer, pick up a book and read it.

His mother is a college English professor married to another college English professor. A boy who is being raised by two college English professors should have a deep and profound love of the written word. But the boy says he doesn't like to read, he hates Language Arts, he hates books and having to write book reports about them. "I think reading is a waste of time," he says.

The boy is so different from boys I grew up with, from my rough-and-tumble brothers, from *boy* as I thought I understood the word. This boy doesn't like to be sweaty, he doesn't like to get dirty. He doesn't like to play sports except for Madden NFL on Xbox 360. He says words like "flash memory" and "firmware dump" and "removable hard drive"; he made a video of himself downgrading 2.6 to 1.5 on his PSP that is over six minutes long; he says he has a bunch of illegal games and stuff he got off the Internet. "If I died and they searched my PSP, they'd know," he says, "but they'd need a warrant."

The boy doesn't run. His walk is plodding, pokey, he drags his feet. He doesn't like to hurry. He has a bike and knows how to ride it, but he'd rather not. Riding a bike means going outside. He doesn't like leaving his room. When I asked him if he thought he might be agoraphobic, a thirteen-year-old agoraphobic, did he think he needed help because I can get him help, he told me that was a mean thing to say.

"You're mean," he said. "A mean woman is my mother. Can you get me help for that?"

A t two-seventeen this morning, Louis and the boy were playing Halo on Xbox 360. I could hear them talking. I don't think they were having a conversation, exactly. They didn't seem to be talking to each other. Their voices were pitchy falsettos. What they were saying creeped me out.

"Mother?" the boy said. "Oh, Mother!"

"Eep!" said Louis. "Eeeep!"

"Why, Mother? Why?" the boy shrilled. "Oh, Mother!"

I don't think he meant me. I think he was talking about some other mother, the universal mother, the one every boy has to turn his back to if he's to become a man.

"This game is so violent, Mother!" the boy harped. "Why are you letting me play such a violent video game, Mother? Mother? Mother!"

Maybe the problem is I can't spread a blanket across the living room floor and put him there. He's too wiggly. He gets up and walks around. Pokes his head in the refrigerator. Pours himself some Mountain Dew. He settles on the couch, then he's on the phone, then he's rooting through the junk drawer looking for a deck of cards or a fishing lure or that great big ball of rubber bands he made back in fourth grade. He says he's hungry and he needs a ride.

The boy is a bleeding heart when it comes to choosing favorites on game shows: if two contestants are white guys and one contestant is a black guy, the boy will root for the black guy every single time. If you ask him isn't it kind of weird to like someone just because he's black, the boy will ask if you're a racist. If you say something snarky about all the blue-hairs at the grocery, it must be Senior Citizen Discount Thursday, the boy will ask if you're ageist.

The boy has strong feelings about hate. He uses the word a lot. He hates people who call attention to themselves. He hates to be the center of attention. He just can't stand to have a lot of people looking at him. He hates even the idea of people thinking about him. He hates pancakes, the way a new car smells, and the feel of newspaper. He says newspaper feels cheap. He hates Jon Bon Jovi, he hates when the temperature rises above seventy-five degrees, he hates generic macaroni and cheese. He hates pierced ears on men, and sometimes, just to mess with his head, I tell him get in the car, we're going to the mall to get your ears pierced.

"I'm not a junkie, Mom," he says.

The boy has still never said he hates me. I've been waiting for him to say it, but he hasn't said it. I keep waiting and waiting. Why hasn't he said it?

I expect he will sooner or later. I'm ready for it, I'm prepared. It won't be a surprise. And when he does, I know what I will say in return:

What the hell do you want from me now?

I'm sorry! I'm sorry! I'm sorry!

I adore you.

Officer Frenchie

When a state trooper passes me on the highway, I grit my teeth, check my speed, and hope nobody put a dead guy in the trunk while I was in Wal-Mart last night at two a.m. When a squad car pulls up behind me at the red light on Front Street and Second, I nervously keep watch in my rearview mirror. Even though I'm pretty sure I've done nothing wrong, committed no crime, I'm wearing my seat belt, I came to a complete stop at that stop sign, I slowed down to twenty miles per hour in that school zone, my insurance is paid, my tags are up-to-date, I used my turn signal and my headlights are in working order, I still feel anxious. Guarded. Uptight. I still say *Oh, great, it's the cops* or *It's the fucking cops* or *Watch out for the fucking pig cops* like I am Bonnie in the getaway car, smoking a cigarette while waiting with toe-tapping impatience for Clyde to get his ass out of that bank, overstuffed bags of cash in his hand. Even though I am almost always completely innocent, I am still not crazy about the police.

Some girls are. Some girls dig cops. It's the uniform, the gun, the nightstick. It's the shiny badge, the way it glints in the light. It catches your eye. It's the promise of power and safety and protection and masculinity, the boy in blue, the crime fighter, the one who goes after the bad guys, the one who kicks ass. Yes, there are little honeys out there who love a cop.

So says the cop who is also my baby brother. His name is Travis, but since childhood, he's been known as Bye-Bye. He's just returned from an all-expenses-paid vacation to Laguna Beach, California, with some little honey who's got a thing for cops.

Bye-Bye has called me up to tell me all about it. I've been on the phone with him for an hour already, listening to his Californian adventure. He wants to know how do you say "X-rated" in French.

The little honey's father is a B-list Hollywood celebrity; she and my brother met two weeks ago, but apparently she's had her eye on him for longer than that. She'd seen him around when he was on bike patrol. Honeys like bike patrol, he says. Girls want to give him their phone number, want to take him out to dinner, or make him dinner, or get into his pants, or crawl into his bed. He says he has to be careful, because honeys are horny and he is the hive. "They want me," he says. "They just can't help themselves." When he's on bike patrol, Bye-Bye's uniform is a department-issued navy blue shirt and navy blue shorts. His badge shines like a diamond, but it's those shorts that catch the female eye. "I can't help I look so good," he says. "I'm just doing my job."

. . .

I was five and a half years old when Bye-Bye was born, and aside from a clear memory of taking his hospital picture to first grade for Show and Tell so I could stand cutely in front of the class, toss-ing my hair and generally showing off, I don't remember his early years at all. I don't remember my mother being pregnant with him. I don't remember my mother going to the hospital so he could be born. I don't remember her bringing home a baby. I don't remem-ber anyone even talking about a baby.

I feel like I should remember something. Especially since there's quite a bit I do remember about the year Bye-Bye was born. It was 1976. "Afternoon Delight" played on the radio fifty times a day. The Supreme Court ruled on *Gregg v. Georgia*, and the Ramones released their self-titled debut album. The United Kingdom broke off diplomatic relations with Uganda, and like every American who was between the ages of five and twelve on July 4, 1976, I have pleasant memories of participating in the celebration concert extravaganza that my hometown put on to honor our nation's bicentennial. I can still feel the scratchy polyester of the blue jumpsuit I wore, the lacy collar on the white blouse, the little red jacket. A white plastic hat completed the look. It kept sliding off my head during the performance but I nonetheless felt adorable. I also felt proud to be an American. I can still belt out every word to such patriot classics as "I'm a Yankee Doodle Dandy" and "When Johnny Comes Marching Home" and "You're a Grand Old Flag."

But I don't remember any baby at my house in 1976.

I don't have a memory of Bye-Bye until he's six years old, then boom! All of a sudden and out of nowhere, there he is, another little brother, a wild boy everyone calls Bye-Bye because he likes to flush the toilet and wave so-long-see-ya-good-bye to its contents.

I already had one brother who was cuter than me; now I had one who was more clever.

In my first memory of him, Bye-Bye is standing on the front stoop of our house. It's late summer, the sun is golden, and the smell of my mother's roses is almost overwhelming. Bye-Bye is stripping off his clothes, he's gyrating his pelvis. He's bumping and grinding and thrusting like he's auditioning for a gig with the Chippendales or the leading role of plumber / porn star. He's grinning, devious and self-satisfied. This has got to be something he's seen on HBO, and though I have overheard our parents whisper to each other that HBO is not appropriate for children, Bye-Bye has watched HBO. A lot. All those times he so sweetly fell asleep on our mother's lap and she was too tired or too lazy or too hypnotized by the tawdriness that was HBO to carry him to his bed, Bye-Bye was really wide-awake. He was watching HBO and here are the consequences.

Bye-Bye is naked on the front stoop, shaking his stuff. Our mother isn't around during this, and I have no idea where she is, but I'm sure she instructed me to watch him. She no doubt said keep an eye on your baby brother. That would be why I'm in such a tizzy about Bye-Bye's burlesque show. I'm worried that even though he's the one naked on the front stoop, his body brown, his penis pink, his butt white, I'm going to be the one who gets in trouble. I can still hear myself telling him, asking him, begging him, "Bye-Bye, please, put your clothes back on, please, please, before somebody sees you," but he keeps dancing naked on the front stoop. He's doing a kind of hula dance that morphs into the hustle. "Please, Bye-Bye? Please put your clothes back on?"

He says no. He won't. And you can't make him. Nobody can.

Nobody will be able to make Bye-Bye do anything he doesn't want to do. Not when he's in second grade and smoking Winstons. Not when he's egging the principal's car in fifth grade or chugging beer in seventh or skipping school in ninth. He gets in trouble with teachers, he gets suspended from school, he gets in fights, once even beating up a kid for saying your mother is a whore. It would seem that juvie is in my brother's future, but he gets through high school, and he goes to college on a football scholarship, and when he drops out after only one semester, nobody is surprised. When he becomes a bouncer at a strip club, nobody is surprised. Nobody is surprised when he stays out partying all night, or when he crashes his motorcycle, or when he dates girls who have stage names, or when he has a tattoo etched on his biceps that he says is a tribal something or other though I think it looks a lot like barbed wire, agricultural fencing to keep the cows in the pasture.

It would seem my littlest brother is headed for a life of bad boy–ness, becoming an enforcer for a Chicago mob family, perhaps, or a white rapper. But when he decides to go to the police academy, to become a crime fighter, a law enforcer, a George W. Bush–supporting Republican, I can't say anybody is surprised. Who better to keep the order than someone who spent so much time thwarting it?

Male pattern baldness runs in our family, and Bye-Bye is among its unfortunate victims. He deals with this genetic injustice by keeping his head shaved, which makes his eyes look enormous, his forehead, huge. Like if he head-butted you even lightly, your skull would crack open like an egg. At five-feet-seven-and-three-quarters, my brother isn't tall, but he's wide and he's solid. He weighs one pound over two hundred. His body fat is 4.7 percent. He works out five days a week, for an hour and a half to two hours, a workout that's carefully planned: chest and cardio and abs on Monday; shoulders, traps, and abs on Tuesday; calves and cardio and abs on Wednesday; shoulders, forearms, cardio, and abs on Thursday; biceps, triceps, cardio, and abs on Friday. He can bench-press more than four hundred pounds. He wears a gold necklace from which dangle two of what he calls pendants and I call charms: one is a bodybuilder lifting a barbell over his head; the other is the number 42.

Bye-Bye likes to look good. He has twenty-five pairs of shoes, he has beautiful silk ties and a gold watch, he has well-fitting suits. He also has a T-shirt that says *Things Not to Say to a Police Officer* and the list includes "Oink! Oink!" "Aren't you the guy from the Village People?" "Gee, Officer, your eyes look glazed—have you been eating doughnuts?" and "No, *you* assume the position."

He was wearing that T-shirt the last time I saw him. Because we live so far apart, we don't get to see much of each other, and I wanted the time we could be together to be special. That night while we were out for dinner, he drew a picture of an enormous speckled and spurting penis on my address book; then he said it's ridiculous that I still make my son go to bed by a certain time; then he told me a joke about a man with a sunburnt dick, how the guy had been advised to dip his dick in milk, and how when he was in the midst of doing so, the man's girlfriend, a dull-witted blonde, said, "I always wondered how you guys loaded those."

My brother knows hundreds of similar jokes. At least twice a week, he calls to tell me them. During these calls, he also describes his love life and mocks my parenting skills. Sometimes I wonder why he would call me. I don't seem to be his audience. I have never been even mildly amused by one of his jokes, I'm defensive about my parenting skills, squeamish about his love life, and alarmed by his sexism. So we don't have much in common. Right now, Bye-Bye is telling me that same joke: the one about the man who stayed out in the sun too long—only this time the guy has been advised to dip his dick in yogurt, and the blonde wants to know if it's fat-free.

My brother is partial to blondes. He comes home from a night at the bar with matchbooks, cocktail napkins, and scraps of paper upon which all the little honeys have written their phone numbers. There are so many blondes that he can't keep them all straight. He needed some way to distinguish them besides the color of their hair so he developed a system of shorthand: *R-Bl-BT*, for example, or *Y-Br-VBT*. The first category is the color of the girl's shirt, *R* meaning red, *Y* meaning yellow. The second—*Bl* and *Br*—notes the color of her eyes, blue and brown, respectively. "I better not even have to tell you what *BT* and *VBT* stand for," he says.

I tell my brother I'm not stupid. "Bright teeth," I say, "and Very Bright Teeth." When he tells me wrong, guess again, I say, "Big Trees" and "Very Big Trees."

And that's all it takes to get him going. He's off, he's running, I've been on the phone with him for two hours, and now it will be two more. He's attacking my politics—"You're all about saving trees but putting serial killers back on the streets," he says. "Aren't you?"—which leads to him attacking my position on the war in Iraq—"I say we just bomb those fuckers, but you're all about giving the terrorists the soft kind of toilet paper and fresh goat meat, aren't you?"—which leads to him attacking my apparent lack of taste—"Chicken livers are delicious, but you don't know what's good, do you? Your taste buds are fried like your brain." He tells me he has undeniable, indisputable proof that marijuana is a gateway drug. "You think dope should be legal and dopers should have drive-thru windows, but you haven't read the studies," he says. "Because you're a pothead." Then he tells me the story about when he held a twelve-year-old in his arms, a boy who would eventually die from the gunshot wound to his neck, the kid popped during a home invasion gone wrong, a botched robbery where the perpetrator was out for the stash belonging to the kid's mother.

"Poor little bastard," my brother says. This isn't the first time or even the second or the third he's told me about it. "Poor little fucker," my brother says. He tells me to hold on a minute, and I hear loud rustling, like he's crumpling newspaper or a plastic grocery bag into the receiver. It's not hard to imagine Bye-Bye is inserting a plug of Copenhagen between his lower lip and gum, or flicking a booger across the room, or catching a fly in his fist, or asking a little honey what time is it. When the rustling stops and he returns, it's to lobby for loosening the restrictions on my son's bedtime. "Look," Bye-Bye says, "you're the one who wants to free criminals and support terrorists and smoke dope, so why are you such a bitch to your own kid? Just tell him, dude, if you're gonna be a mean little asshole because you're tired from staying up all night, I'ma gonna sticka my foot up ya ass. You baby that kid. How long are you going to let him dangle from your tit? It's time to get a stick and beat him with it. Sister, you got to tell him get off my tit, you little sucker! Let go!"

Next to the picture of the speckled dick my brother drew in my address book, he wrote a 42 and put a circle around it—the number on his high school football jersey. My brother voted for George W. Bush, not once, but twice, and he told me he'd do what I think is unimaginable, inconceivable, unfathomable, and irresponsible: "I'd vote for my man a third time if I could. Hell, yeah!" When he vacationed with that B-list celebrity's daughter in California, he showed her some love on Friday night, and apparently she was a kinky sex freak, because afterward she said she wanted to introduce him to her best friend—"Another kinky sex freak!"—and on Saturday night and for part of the day on Sunday, the three of them did like they were French.

"I bet you don't know what I'm talking about, do you?" he says. My brother is so crude and nasty and arrogant, and I don't always believe the things he tells me, maybe because I don't want to. But he is also the only person in my life who has never hung up the telephone without first saying he loves me.

I've been on the phone with him for three hours; hanging up is still another hour away. When I tell him, "Travis, you are disgusting," he sings in a high-pitched voice, "Kinky sex freaks," then in his regular voice he says he wishes he knew a nice girl, he asks me do I know any nice girls, do I know any nice girls I could introduce him to, any nice girls he could meet?

Sufficiently

Suffonsified

When I went to Detroit to visit Al's family, I got a glimpse into what he and I might become, what our future might look like. In it, Al dozes in his La-Z-Boy while I watch made-for-TV movies from mine: I'm especially partial to ones where Melissa Gilbert or Valerie Bertinelli plays a woman who's been victimized by the patriarchy and how she overcomes that oppression. During commercials, Al snores, and I check out the home shopping on QVC, maybe catch Joan Rivers hawking her line of baubles. When Al wakes up, we chain-smoke, express skepticism about the severity of the other's back pain, and call up family members to ask how much they pay for goods and services like milk and gasoline and long distance.

In short, we become my in-laws.

I didn't want to go to Detroit.

Al's eighty-one-year-old father, Lucky, and seventy-six-year-old stepmother, Karleen, live in a suburb on the east side. Because

Al doesn't seem to understand that the secret to the family visit is staying in a hotel, they provide our accommodations. Their guest room is Al's childhood bedroom, the place where, according to Al, the magic began.

It's fine with me that he wants to visit his folks. I never try to stop him. In his absence, I can keep myself entertained: there are puppet show / craft activities at the public library, for example, and regularly scheduled free lessons on how to tie woolly boogers and sow bugs at Check Your Fly, and the ongoing seventy-five-percent-off sale at the local porn store.

The first time I ever met Al's dad was just a day or two after the old man's heart surgery. Lucky was still in the hospital, recovering, fragile, and pale, when he asked Al to bring him a hand mirror, a hairbrush, and a large chocolate shake from McDonald's. Vain and sweet-toothed, Lucky was my kind of guy, and later that day, Karleen, his wife, gave me two Xanax, which in my book made her A-okay.

Lucky had been home from the hospital for less than an hour when he asked if Al and I would do him a favor. The man had survived some intense medical stuff; we were happy to accommodate him. "Anything!" we said.

He wanted us to buy toilet paper. He was particular about what he wanted—Charmin Plus with Lotion, a twelve-pack—and he was clear about where we were to make this purchase: "I want you to go to the Kmart on Gratiot."

There were already three twelve-packs of Charmin Plus with Lotion in the linen closet, and though Al and I agreed that nine rolls for each of us ought to be plenty, we didn't see anything wrong with humoring him.

But when I suggested we walk to the little mom-and-pop grocery down the street instead of driving several miles to Kmart, Al said no. He said they probably didn't carry Charmin Plus with Lotion. When I said we could see if they did, he said why bother, it would be cheaper at Kmart. When I offered to cough up the difference, saying it couldn't be that much more, and even if it amounted to twenty dollars, I'd be happy to pay it as a way to avoid going to Kmart, Al said thank you, but that would not be necessary.

"The toilet paper will be purchased at Kmart," he said. "It's what my father wants."

Such inflexibility from the guy who once went out for a loaf of bread and came home with a two-thousand-dollar acoustic-electric guitar was hard to understand. I asked how would his father know whether we bought the toilet paper at Kmart or Wal-Mart, Target or Meijer. If we heisted a twelve-pack of Charmin Plus with Lotion from a shipment en route to South America or won it in a game of dice from some back-alley pusher, really, how would the old man possibly know, and even if he did discover the truth, so what? It's not like he could ground us. It's not like he could take away our phone privileges or deny us the keys to the car for a month.

Al looked at me sadly. "You were real wild as a teenager, weren't you?" he said. "I bet you told a lot of lies." He decided to go to Kmart without me. Like it was a punishment.

Still, I understood where Al was coming from. Going home means regressing to the boy whose job is to take out the trash or the girl who sets the table. No matter how old you are, home is the place where the grown-ups still get to decide what's on TV and when it's lights-out. If they let you borrow the car, they want to know where are you going, when will you be back. Going home means going back in time. It's not a trip you care to take alone, and anyway, isn't that the main reason to take a mate? So you have an ally in the civil war against your parents?

Out-of-town visitors do not justify a deviation from my in-laws' routine. The last time we were there, Al and I put our suitcase in the guest room, we sat down on the bumpy couch, we watched a movie starring either Melissa Gilbert or Valerie Bertinelli on Lifetime Television. Al's stepmother immediately returned to the topic she discussed at length the last time I was there: everything she hates about Al's father.

"I just don't know about that man!" Karleen said. She was wearing a pink velour tunic top with dragonflies embroidered around the collar. "I think there's something wrong with him!" she said. She was talking about the amount of time Lucky spends in the bathroom, which, according to her, is a lot. "Guess what he's doing in there!" she said.

We said we couldn't begin to.

"Why, he's primping! He's combing his hair! Fixing it just so!" she said. "He's worse than a woman!"

Karleen also resented that Lucky falls asleep in his La-Z-Boy every night by eight o'clock. "It's lonely!" she said. "I don't have anybody to talk to." She found it irritating that he's always fussing, obsessively straightening, stacking, tidying, cleaning. Apparently, he scoured the enamel off the bathtub, scrubbed right down to the steel. "What's wrong with him?" Karleen wanted to know. Then she announced she didn't believe for a minute that Lucky's hearing is as bad as he makes it out to be. "Trust me," she said, "he can hear when he wants to."

Lucky was sitting in his La-Z-Boy, nodding like he could indeed hear what his wife had been saying about him, every word of it, and he was smiling like he agreed. "How much was your last electric bill, Allen?" he said, and when Al told him it was one hundred and twenty-nine dollars, Karleen shouted, "IT WAS ONE HUNDRED AND TWENTY-NINE DOLLARS!" and Lucky said, "Uh-huh. Uh-huh."

Lucky's hearing loss began with a case of childhood measles, and over the years it's gotten progressively worse. He's now ninety percent deaf. About ten years ago, he signed up to learn lip-reading at a local community center, but he only went to a class or two before dropping out. He didn't say why. Having a conversation with him over the telephone is next to impossible, so Al sometimes writes his father letters, but Lucky doesn't answer them. It's like playing catch with someone who won't toss back the ball. When Al asked him did you get my letters, the old man said he did. Then he asked Al how much does he pay for a pound of hamburger.

It always catches me by surprise just how much Al and his father are alike. If I want a sneak peek of Al at age eighty, all I have to do is take a look at his old man. Lucky's ears are big and stick out. His glasses are big and round, his teeth are not his own. Though his appetite is gluttonous, he has always been a slender man. He hitches up his corduroy pants past his navel, then belts them so they stay there, high as if for a flood. He wears his shirts tucked in, his shoes in the house, navy blue cotton pajamas to bed. He's four inches shorter than he used to be, but Lucky is still a handsome man, blue-eyed and smooth-skinned, proud of his hair, which is thick and full, silvery gray and parted on the right. On top, his hair swirls into two distinct finger waves, like silver surf on a moonlit beach, a stage prop on loan from *The Lawrence Welk Show*. In his hospital room, any time someone asked him how was he feeling, heart surgery is serious, was he feeling okay, Lucky would apologize for his hair. "It probably looks just terrible," he said. "I hate to think how it must look."

"The Silver Fox," Karleen calls him. She rinses her own hair with Miss Clairol #20 Arctic Blonde. Lucky is her second husband; she is his second wife. Though they've been married for fifteen years, each plans to be buried next to his or her original spouse. Of her first husband, Karleen says, "He was a decent man and a hard worker. Unlike some people," she adds, as if to suggest Lucky needs to put down the crack pipe, get off his duff, and hang some drywall, as if she's forgotten there was an article in the newspaper about how Lucky is a decent man, how he found a purse in the street that contained several hundred dollars, and instead of tossing the purse and sliding the cash into his pocket, instead of thinking of it as free money, Lucky turned it over to the police.

When I asked Al if he would have done the same, he said probably. But that's also what he said when I asked him if he'd eat the dog if he was hungry and there was nothing else he could eat, and when I asked him if I died before he did, would he ever have sex again.

Probably.

But Lucky doesn't live in a world of probably. Lucky is all about definitely. You turn in a purse full of money because it's the right thing to do. You remain married to a woman who berates you, you pay your debt. You don't look back. You don't talk about the infant daughter who died, or that you didn't appreciate your first wife until after she was dead; you don't mention the grandson who died; you don't talk about the job you didn't take or the chance you didn't take, or any of the ways your life might have been different, better, bigger. Because what good does it do to talk about it?

What Lucky wants is simple: a glass of milk with his supper, and after supper, he wants a cup of decaf and a piece of pie; and after that, he wants a cigarette. Lucky wants a bowl of ice cream while he's watching television. He wants for people to be happy, and for people to be nice, and for people to get along. Everyone but Karleen thinks he's a sweet old guy.

"Uh-huh," he says. "Uh-huh."

The reason he doesn't like to talk about the past probably has something to do with how messy it is, how it's something he can't disinfect or straighten up or rearrange. A retired school janitor, Lucky wants structure and order and routine. The custodian's closets and storage rooms at his school were immaculate; he keeps his house just as tidy. No dust, no clutter, nothing out of place.

"I just can't stand the mess," he says, and his son is the same way. Last Christmas morning, I woke up early to the noise of Al running the vacuum cleaner, Al squeaking the mop across the kitchen floor, Al wearing rubber gloves and scouring the sink. Oh my God, I'd said. What is wrong with you? It's Christmas. Don't start with the cleaning.

Karleen patted my hand. "Oh, honey," she said. "It will only get worse!" She lit up a Virginia Slim 100. With smoke swirling around her face, she looked wise. She also looked pleased, like she was glad to be delivering the bad news. It meant she wasn't alone. "Just you wait!" she said. Then she described for me my future. It included doilies under the milk jug in the refrigerator and Al hovering outside the bathroom door, wearing a pair of rubber gloves and waiting for me to finish up my business so he could rush in there with a bottle of pine-scented Lysol.

"If the son is anything like the father," she said, "your life is not going to be easy."

Karleen and I looked at Lucky, asleep in his La-Z-Boy, and in his face, there is Al's: the rectangular shape, the wide forehead, the blunt chin. Father and son look so much alike, except the son weighs about twenty pounds more. When Al returned to the living room with a piece of pie, Lucky, who hadn't said much since his inquiry into the price of laundry detergent, said, "My goodness, Allen, you sure are fat. Why are you so fat? I've never seen you this fat."

After the Melissa Gilbert / Valerie Bertinelli movie, Karleen changed the channel to QVC. The merchandise that can be purchased on that station—the Diamonique tennis bracelets and mock-neck jackets with the metallic-bead detail, the pink palace chandelier earrings (designed by Joan Rivers) and the vanilla-scented battery-operated candles—never fails to amaze me. For a certain segment of the population, QVC is a lot like porn: the soft lights, the hyped-up enthusiasm, the I-got-to-get-me-some-of-that response it provokes in the viewer. Lucky and Karleen watch a lot of QVC.

But one of them doesn't stop with watching.

Karleen has herself a nasty little addiction to buying stuff she will never use. Everyone seems to know about it, but nobody talks about it, about how she ratcheted up forty thousand dollars on their Discover card because she can't stop herself from dialing the toll-free number and buying whatever. An exercise bike. A wrought-iron umbrella stand. A vehicle snow kit with a heated ice scraper (it plugs into your car's cigarette lighter), snow brush, and shovel. Her shopping addiction distresses Lucky: Last summer, he fretted silently and to himself about how on earth they're ever going to pay their Discover card bill, until he ended up in the hospital with shingles—aggravated by stress, the doctor said—but he seems powerless to stop her, while she seems powerless to stop herself. When I suggested to Al that maybe she's just trying to get his attention, maybe it is lonely when you have no one to talk to, maybe it's incredibly irritating to open the refrigerator and find that your husband has placed a doily under the milk, he wanted to know was I empathizing with Karleen?

Whose side was I on?

While Karleen commented from her easy chair on whether or not she liked a particular product and why or why not, I did what I always do when I don't know what else to do: I kissed ass. I smiled, I nodded, I agreed. Lucky, sitting in his easy chair, his feet up and his hands folded across his belly, snoozed.

But Al sighed. Al stood up, he sat down, he looked around the room. Al looked at his hands, his feet, the space between his feet. He stared into space. When he straightened up a pile of newspaper that was already in a tidy pile, Karleen said, "Look at him. He's like his father. He can't sit still. He's always got to be messing with something. There's something wrong with both of them."

Al said he did not know what a goose-down pillow costs at a store in our town, but the price of the goose-down pillow QVC host Bob Bowersox was pushing seemed like a good deal, though the call-in testimonials seemed too gung-ho to be real. Al looked at his watch, he chewed on his thumbnail. Ten minutes went by, then twenty, then twenty more. Al stood, stretched, groaned, then he shuffled down the hall, first into our room, then toward the bathroom. I heard him brushing his teeth.

On QVC, a blond former beauty queen prattled on about a velour tunic-and-pants set. This outfit came in five rich, gemlike colors (emerald, sapphire, amethyst, peridot, and ruby). You can wear it anywhere! she chipperly pointed out. How dressy, sassy, and comfy you would be in this outfit, and because of the rhine-stones along the neckline and sleeves, how sparkly. It seemed like all of the tunics (V-neck, asymmetrical, crinkle georgette, stretch waffle, chiffon, bell-sleeved, long-sleeved, long-sleeved with side slits, long-sleeved pucker-knit raglan) were decorated (with rhine-stone details, beadwork, embroidery, rhinestone snowflakes, drag-onfly sparkles, glitter, crotchet trim, scattered rhinestones, faux fur, gold-tone sequins, fairy dust). It seemed like all of the coor-dinating pants had an elastic waistband. I'd always heard elastic referred to as the devil's measuring tape, and because I was alone with Al's parents, and I felt weird and awkward and uncomfort-able, and I couldn't think of anything else to say, I said this.

"What's that?" said Lucky, snapping awake.

"SHE SAYS YOUR SON NEEDS AN ELASTIC WAIST-BAND!" Karleen shouted. "BECAUSE HE'S SO FAT!"

Lucky shook his head. "I don't know," he said, "why he got fat."

How many times had Al described this house to me? So many that it felt familiar, I felt like I'd grown up in it, too. There was the kitchen table where, night after night, every night, four-year-old

Al spilled his milk. There was the dining room where nine-year-old Al drew pictures that disturbed his mother because they were pictures of naked ladies with two circles for their breasts, two dots for nipples. There was the spot on the living room floor where ten-year-old Al played with plastic Army guys. I could almost see him setting them up then knocking them down then setting them up again.

I could hear fifty-five-year-old Al calling to me, urgently stage whispering my name. "C'mere, c'mere, c'mere," he whispered. He was peeking out from the guest room, the room that used to be his bedroom, the bedroom where fourteen-, sixteen-, seventeen-year-old Al pumped the python, buffed the banana, and played flute solos while thinking about Sophia Loren, imagining himself wooing Sophia Loren, offering her a single red rose, a box of chocolates, his hand, picturing Sophia Loren guiding his hand to her breast (a circle with a dot). His Sophia Loren fantasies were something else I'd heard about a million times before. Al's old bedroom is now a claustrophobic space with a sleeper sofa and framed photographs of Karleen's children and grandchildren and great-grandchildren, a progression of age that begins at infancy and culminates with high school graduation hangs from floor to ceiling.

"C'mere, c'mere, c'mere," Al was whispering. I murmured excuse me to my hosts, who were watching young women model outfits for old women, this time a gingham shirt and capri pants set embroidered with pineapples, ladybugs, daisies, cherries, or palm trees, your choice. As I approached, Al reached out, took my hand, and tugged me into the room.

"Hello there," he said. He embraced me then slipped his hand in my shirt and started feeling me up. "Those old people are driving me crazy!" he said. Al said he had a plan. Very soon, we would take the old people out for dinner, somewhere nice, somewhere fun, somewhere where we could have a drink. "You deserve a drink!" he said. "You deserve two drinks!" But first, Al said, before we did anything else, he sort of felt like fooling around. Did I want to fool around? "Come on," he said, inching one hand up my shirt and the other down my pants. "What do you say? Let's you and me fool around."

We emerged from the guest room ravenous. Lucky said he could order a pizza. He suggested Little Caesars. He had a coupon that he'd clipped out of the phone book which would save us a few bucks, plus they'd deliver it right to our door, isn't that handy? "I like to stay close to home," Lucky told us. He lived twelve miles from downtown, but hadn't been there in years. "I can't even tell you what's downtown anymore."

"I'll tell you what's downtown," Karleen said. "*Black people.*"

Lucky said but if we were going to insist on going out to eat, he didn't want to go anyplace too fancy like Applebee's or Red Lobster, which are also too expensive. He'd be okay to eat supper at Ram's Horn, a family-style restaurant franchise across southern Michigan. There was one only two miles from the house, and, according to Lucky, they had good fish and chips, taco salad, turkey dinner with all the fixings, really good pie, and chicken Parmesan.

Ram's Horn it is!

Before we left, I wanted to brush my teeth, but I'd forgotten to pack my toothbrush. When I'd asked Al if I could borrow his, he said no. He said sharing a toothbrush was disgusting.

"It seems unhygienic," he said.

Never mind what we did in his childhood bedroom while his father and stepmother sat in their easy chairs watching QVC. Al was repulsed by the idea of his toothbrush in my mouth. "Rub some toothpaste on with your finger," he said, "but can you make it snappy? My father is waiting."

My worst experience with food poisoning happened because of a gyro I ate at a street carnival in Syracuse, New York. I should have known better as I'd been made violently ill by gyros before and would be again. In fact, every single time I've ever eaten a gyro I got stomach-churning sick, but I keep coming back for more, thinking this time it will be different. When it comes to seasoned lamb cooked on a rotisserie, sliced in slivers, slathered with that white sauce, buried under tomatoes and onions, then swaddled in a warm, soft, chewy pita, mine is a piggy appetite made even piggier by the fact that I live in a town where there is not a single Greek restaurant.

I ordered a gyro at Ram's Horn served with French fries and cole slaw, though instead of a handsome moustached man named Nikos shouting hey have some more ouzo, *oopa!* have some delicious baklava, Amber the Waitress stood cranelike on one foot, scratching the back of her leg with the other while asking did I need ketchup. Al sat across from me, wiggling his eyebrows, and licking his tongue across his lips, and winking in an exaggerated way. He seemed to be enjoying himself.

So did my father-in-law. Lucky is fun to share a meal with. He loves the food in front of him, no matter how simple, no matter how bland, and if you're sitting next to him at Ram's Horn, you'll hear him emit a series of low soft Mmmmmms, his reaction to bites of something delicious, the last taste every bit as good as the first.

But he is color-blind. Sixty-some years of smoking Winston Lights have fouled up his sense of smell. He has arthritis. Maybe food is so delicious because his gustatory system is picking up all the slack, his taste buds working time and a half. He says Mmmmm about his daily bowl of instant oatmeal or his serving of canned cream-style corn or the dish of strawberry Jell-O they gave him for dessert when he was in the hospital.

He said Mmmmm about the slice of white bread that came with his meal at Ram's Horn; otherwise, it was silent. Karleen picked up a fried shrimp, nibbled once or twice, put it down, then repeated the procedure on another. While I sucked on ice from my Diet Pepsi, Al rubbed his foot against my leg. He'd ordered the fish-and-chips, but he hardly touched it. Instead, he was intent on playing footsie with me.

I kicked him away.

There was something wrong with that man.

At Ram's Horn, he slid off his shoe and poked and prodded his foot around in my lap. I shoved him off me. "Stop it," I hissed. "I'm not kidding." My stomach was starting to churn. Was it in response to the gyro or was it concern that this—this—was my future? That Al would become as fussy as his old man and I would turn bitter like Karleen and together we'd live a life of silent meals and scorn? It infuriated me that he wouldn't let me use his toothbrush.

"Mmmmmm," Lucky said. "Mmmmmm."

He chopped his spaghetti into bits then scooped them up on his fork. After he wiped his plate clean with a piece of bread, Lucky pressed his lips together and dabbed his napkin against the corners of his mouth in a deliberate and pompous way. Smiling at us, he announced, "My sufficiency has been suffonsified."

Spoken in a haughty tone, that phrase means I'm full, I'm stuffed, I couldn't eat another bite, and I've heard only one other person say it. Al says it after a dinner of pot roast and mashed potatoes, or tuna casserole with crushed-potato-chip topping, or a turkey and all the trimmings prepared in the month of June just to please him. "My sufficiency has been suffonsified," Al says, and I also have started saying, "Any further indulgence would be super-sanctimonious." It's the language of this family.

Later that night, when my stomach knotted and cramped up on itself—it probably was the gyro—Al and I were alone on the sofa bed in his old bedroom. He gave me a Tums, he brought me a glass of milk, he rubbed my back.

"I was thinking," he said. "We can always run over to Kmart and buy you a toothbrush. Why don't we do that?"

That's when I asked him what I'd been worrying about since we got here. I asked him was he going to turn into his father. He said probably. He said he probably already had.

It's Me. It's Him.

It's Them.

It may just be me.

I worry that my friend Andrew Boyle is a pervert, even if he doesn't hang fuzzy dice from the rearview mirror of a sleekly black Pontiac Trans Am. Andrew doesn't own a Trans Am or a customized van all decked out with zebra-skin rug, water bed, and a sign that reads IF YOU SEE THIS VAN A-ROCKIN', DON'T COME A-KNOCKIN'. He doesn't linger in front of the Kwik Trip where the troubled high school girls—the pukers, the cutters, the partiers, the sluts—like to hang out smoking cigarettes and drinking Diet Cokes after school. He doesn't unbutton his polyester shirt all the way down to his snakeskin belt. Andrew Boyle fusses over his appearance, he is always fashionably dressed, he purchases his clothes on eBay, designer brands so expensive I've never even heard of them. He doesn't wear polyester shirts. Andrew Boyle wouldn't be caught dead in polyester. Nor does he wear shiny shoes, like the ones the sleazy teacher at your school wore so he could stand close to a cheerleader and sneak peeks up her skirt in the reflection of his shoe. Though he lists *Lolita* as one of his favorite novels, Andrew does not leer at schoolyard nymphets nor does he say *Light of my life, fire of my loins* or *Hey, little girl, do you want some candy?* or *I'm gonna make a big star out of you* except, maybe, as a joke, something he might drunkenly say to a beautiful woman of appropriate age with the hope that she will model for him.

When I was first getting to know Andrew, I didn't think I would like him, because he seemed arrogant and show-offy. And it would turn out that I was right: Andrew Boyle is arrogant and show-offy, but he is also witty and well-read, environmentally conscious and politically aware, a person with whom you can have a smart and interesting conversation about Raymond Carver's short stories or Robert Altman's films or the Canadian rock band Rush or Peter Singer's argument against speciesism. When I like Andrew Boyle, I like him a lot. He can be easily amused, easily entertained; his laugh is nice to hear.

A vegetarian except during Thanksgiving Dinner, Andrew takes good care of himself. He doesn't smoke cigarettes or marijuana, he doesn't chew tobacco or gum or drink cheap domestic beer. He drinks Grenache Shiraz Mourvèdre, vintage 2001. I've never heard of it, but he says it tastes like PBJ without the bread or the peanut butter. He doesn't mind when I call him a snob. He doesn't take offense.

He doesn't have a pierced ear or wear a gold medallion on a gold chain. He does have a gold watch that his parents gave him for a graduation present, an expensive gold watch from a fine watchmaker, but because gold jewelry is tacky, he doesn't wear it. When he thinks about his parents giving him this gift of a watch that he'll probably never wear, he feels guilty.

At some angles, Andrew is very handsome; at others, he's sort of funny-looking. Gawky. Geeky. He can look hip and cool and urbane or he can also look like what he is: a dorky high school valedictorian who spent many a Friday night playing Dungeons & Dragons and secretly wishes he still did.

His undergraduate degrees are in math and music. He has a Ph.D. in art history from a prestigious European university. Andrew can affect the world-weary, snobby, snotty, fashionably androgynous attitude of someone who's spent some time hobnobbing in Europe. A friend of mine, upon first meeting him, was surprised to learn that Andrew was not gay. "Of course he is," she said. "He's completely gay. He's totally gay," and when I told her no, he's just serious about the time he spent hobnobbing in Europe, she insisted, "That guy is so gay."

Lots of people assume Andrew Boyle is gay—probably because of his meticulous posture and graceful gesturing, his lack of interest in organized sports, and the jaunty gray scarf he wears indoors wrapped around his neck so the ends dangle over his shoulders and down his chest in a casually studied way. But he's not gay. Andrew Boyle is just the kind of guy who knows about girl stuff. What girls like. What it's like to be a girl. Sometimes the thought occurs to me that he knows more about being a girl than I do, that I've been doing it all wrong. Why don't I get my eyebrows plucked? Why do I still buy my clothes at JCPenney, and how can it be that I haven't ever heard of Marc Jacobs? Why was I so flattered when Andrew Boyle told me he approved of my shoes, cork wedges that take me from barely five feet to five-feet-four?

"Those are great shoes," he said. Then he told me he loved what I'd been doing with my hair. "It looks good. Your hair looks like a shampoo commercial."

"Well, thank you, Andrew!" I said modestly. I was very flattered because usually I don't think about my hair unless it's to hate it. "I usually hate my hair!" I told Andrew Boyle. "It's so thick, it's hard to manage. It's hard to find something to do with it."

"You know what I like to do when a woman has thick hair?" Andrew asked.

"No. What? Tell me."

He slid his hand under my mop of big, thick hair, he grabbed a hunk of it, he yanked, snapping my head back, exposing my neck. "Sexy," he said.

I frowned, but I stayed calm. I took a deep breath, raised my eyebrows. "Well," I said.

But I was furious. Because when Andrew Boyle pulled my hair like that, it hurt like hell. But I was determined not to let him know that. Because I wondered if that's what he wanted. Because I think there's no way it's me: this guy is definitely a pervert. *I bet he's seen that move in a thousand and one pornos*, I thought. *He is such a fucking pervert.* But what made me angriest is at the time I couldn't think of what I could do back. What was some comparable physical action that's equal parts pain and humiliation?

What I came up with, of course, is that someday I will kick Andrew Boyle in the nuts. Hard. When he is least expecting it.

Currently, Andrew is an assistant professor of art history at a midsized state university. According to RateMyProfessors .com, a website that asks college students to comment on their teachers, Dr. Boyle is demanding; a real tough grader; very helpful; boring even though he doesn't think he is; an okay teacher; a great teacher; a total phony; an excellent teacher; hostile to Christianity; extremely open-minded; a guy who loves to hear himself talk; enthusiastic and laid-back; someone who wants everyone to be his pal; and a blowhard who thinks he's better than everybody else.

Andrew Boyle is almost exactly two years older than me. Soon, he will turn thirty-eight. To celebrate his birthday, he'd like his friends to join him for a night on the town. He'd like to have some fun. In the meantime, he wanted to know if I was interested in going out for dinner and drinks with him one night this week. He seemed lonely, and I felt bad for him, but I had to say no. I had to remind him why I don't go out on weeknights. "I've got that kid at home," I told him. "I've got that husband."

"Oh, right," he said. "I forgot." He sighed, loud and sad. "Everybody has a kid at home. Everyone has a family. Everyone except me."

Andrew would like to have a kid at home someday. He'd like to have a wife—he's never had a wife—but right now he doesn't have a girlfriend or even prospects for a girlfriend. He doesn't have a dog or a cat or a houseplant or a house. He lives in a duplex. He says he doesn't have a reason to live. One night last March, Andrew Boyle sat at my kitchen table where he ate five garlic-stuffed olives and drank half a Summit pale ale, then told me he'd been entertaining thoughts of jumping off a bridge. "Pretty much every day," he said. Six months later, he's saying the same thing. In fact, just the day before yesterday he told me he doesn't know why he goes on living. "I have nothing to live for," he said.

What Andrew Boyle does have is a camera. He takes pictures with it, pictures of landscapes sometimes, but more often, when he can find willing models, he takes pictures of women, especially young women of appropriate age (which means they're at least eighteen) who also happen to be beautiful (which means they're thin and bosomy or, as my father would say, "built like a brick shithouse"). These women must also be interested in participating in what Andrew calls art photos (which means they disrobe). Andrew Boyle is always in search of beautiful young women willing to pose naked for him.

In his experience, high-end hair salons are a good source of such young beautiful women. "Hairstylists tend to care about their appearance," he says. "They're interested in beauty. They keep themselves up." Hairstylists, according to Andrew, are frequently vain, a quality he very much approves of, because an appeal to a woman's vanity is often what finally convinces her to model for him. Because you look good, I imagine him saying, you're hot, you're sexy, and well, you know, you're not always going to look like this.

Andrew has also noticed that waitresses at bars in college towns are frequently young and beautiful. One Friday night, I went out for dinner with Andrew, and afterward he suggested we have a drink at The Wooden Nickel, a bar that's well known as a meat market for college kids, the place where after they get good and drunk on Jägermeister and Red Bull, Screaming Orgasms, and six-dollar pitchers of Long Island Iced Teas, they hook up and have sex. Andrew said he knew a waitress there, a girl named Robyn, who was working that night. "I want to invite Robyn to my upcoming birthday festivities," he said. "I also want to ask her if she'll model for me."

Robyn had blond pigtails, blue eyes, dimples, and long legs in knee-high socks. She was wearing shorts. She was wearing high-heeled boots. Her eyebrows were plucked to perfection, her nose was pierced, her ears were double-pierced. She was cute as a pixie, and she knew Andrew by name and drink.

"Hi, Andrew," she said. "Do you want a Summit?"

Andrew said, "Robyn, some friends and I will be celebrating my thirty-eighth birthday next week, and you are invited to join the festivities. My birthday is on a Wednesday night, but most people can't party with me in the middle of the week. So we are going to have the festivities on the weekend. Are you free on Friday night?"

Robyn said she thought she had to work on Friday night.

"Are you free on Saturday night?"

Robyn said she wasn't sure, but she thought she might have to work on Saturday night.

"Let me know," Andrew said.

Robyn told him she would let him know, then she glanced at me. We smiled at each other, tight-lipped smiles, and I understood that this girl might be cute as a pixie but she wasn't stupid, and I knew Robyn the Waitress at The Wooden Nickel would be posing for Andrew on the twelfth of never, and it's not just me. It's him. Other girls feel it, too. Andrew Boyle is most definitely a pervert.

On several occasions Andrew has sat at my kitchen table, opened up his leather satchel, and pulled out a leather-covered portfolio containing his art photos, pictures he took of a beautiful naked woman of appropriate age. Before seeing these pictures, I made fun of Andrew. I said oh yes, *art photos*. I said do you drive a Trans Am? Do you wear shiny shoes? Where is your gold medallion? Are you a pervert? No, really, are you?

However, after seeing the pictures, I had to agree that they were neither dirty nor pornographic. The pictures are beautiful. The woman in the pictures is always beautiful, her body the body of youth, her skin smooth skin, her body a firm but curvy body, nothing is fatty, nothing is drooping.

The woman in the pictures may change, but what remains constant is that she is always someone Andrew had fucked or was fucking or wanted to fuck, and that's something that, for me, keeps them from being art photos, the work of an artist. That's something that, no matter how beautiful they are, turns them into booby pictures that Andrew took and pulled out of a leather satchel as we sat at my kitchen table—pictures that, for reasons I haven't yet figured out, Andrew showed to me but not to my husband, who wandered into the kitchen to fix a ham sandwich while Andrew and I flipped through his leather-covered portfolio—and I tried to think of things to say that weren't "How on earth did you ever talk this girl into doing this?"

Instead, I commented on how many triangles I could find. The bend of a knee is a triangle, and the crook of an elbow. "There are so many triangles in these pictures!" I said. I wondered if it is just me. If I am too much of a prude to appreciate the human body, a woman's body, the beautiful thing that it is. I don't want to be a prude, but maybe I am.

One of the models looked just as good clothed and in person. I know because she ate Thanksgiving dinner at my house last year when she and Andrew were still a couple. Her name was Lauren; she was twenty-one years old, a college junior who had once been Andrew's student, and during the entire turkey celebration, Lauren hardly spoke. She sat at the table with the other guests, but she didn't contribute to any conversation unless a specific question was directed at her. She spoke only to Andrew, and she let Andrew speak for her. I didn't hold this against Lauren then or now: it probably was unnerving to have dinner at a stranger's house, it probably was intimidating, it probably was embarrassing that the person at Thanksgiving dinner closest to your age was the hostess's thirteen-year-old son. It probably took every bit of courage Lauren had to come up to me and say what she said.

What did she say?

I'm still not sure. It came out sounding a lot like chirping. Like tweet! tweet! tweet!

"What?" I asked her.

"Tweet! Tweet! Tweet!" Her voice was high-pitched and squeaky. Like a little bird.

That night, she and Andrew went back to Andrew's duplex, where a "photo shoot" took place.

In December, Andrew spent hundreds of dollars buying her Christmas gifts: designer clothes, silk lingerie, high-heeled boots.

In January, he was talking about marrying her.

By March it was over. Lauren—quite inexplicably, Andrew thought—broke things off. She wouldn't return his calls. She wasn't interested in his broken heart. She may or may not have been involved with someone else, and all Andrew had left was her image on black-and-white film. "I don't understand," he said. He was sitting at my kitchen table with his half a Summit and a jar of garlic-stuffed olives. He looked terrible, unshaven, unshowered, like he hadn't slept in days. I felt really bad for him.

"I'll tell you what I didn't understand," I said, and I did what I thought a friend should do: I bad-mouthed the person who caused him such pain. I told him about Lauren chirping at me on Thanksgiving. "Tweet! Tweet! Tweet! I didn't understand a word of it," I told him.

I thought it would make him feel better, but it didn't. "That's really mean," Andrew said. "You're really catty to talk about her like that. She thought you were so nice. I can't believe how cruel you can be. That's pretty shallow of you."

As a pre-celebration celebration of Andrew Boyle's thirty-eighth birthday, we went to The Wooden Nickel. Andrew and I sat at a table in Robyn's section, and as he watched the little pixie blond waitress serve drinks, he sighed. He said he just knew that people think he's a dullard, that he comes off as a man with a very dull personality. He seemed sincere about this self-perception, he seemed glum. I told him I don't think he's a dullard, which is true, I don't. I said I thought he was a weirdo.

This perked him up. "Really?" he said. "Tell me why!"

I considered telling him I actually think he's more of a pervert than a weirdo, but he was smiling so nicely, expectantly, and I could see the boy in Andrew Boyle, the sweet, smiling kid in blue footy pajamas waking up happy on the morning of his birthday knowing that there would be a cake and lit candles and a chorus of loved ones singing him a birthday song. "The scarf!" I said.

"What scarf?"

"That gray scarf you wear. You take off your coat, but you keep that scarf wrapped around your neck. It's very jaunty. You wear a scarf indoors, Andrew. Where I come from, men don't do that. Men don't wear scarves in a blizzard, let alone indoors."

"I'd get beat up where you come from, wouldn't I?" said Andrew.

Yes, I told him, he would most definitely get beat up. He would get the shit kicked out of him.

He didn't seem insulted or displeased. In fact, he took it more as a compliment. "I guess I'm not very manly," he said. He was scanning the crowd at The Wooden Nickel. He reminded me of myself, examining every chocolate in the box of Whitman's Sampler, wanting the one that was caramel, but convinced someone else had gotten to it first. Andrew fixed his gaze on a beautiful, willowy blond twenty-year-old. "I won't go talk to her," he said, "because I think she won't be interested in me. I mean, what could I say that won't sound like a line?" His shoulders slumped and I resisted the urge to tell him sit up straight! Don't slouch! "I won't ask her for a date," he continued, "but maybe I can ask her to model for me. She won't be interested in dating me, but she might be interested in modeling for me. The point is, I got a girl to talk to me."

Whenever Andrew Boyle follows a woman's name with the words "model for me," I don't know how to feel. Maybe he's not a pervert, maybe he's just a lonely guy, full of self-doubt, worried that he's not good enough for a woman to love, worried that he'll never get married, have a kid, a family, and the camera is something for him to hide behind, that inviting a woman to model for him is a way to strike up a conversation with a woman he'd never dare speak to otherwise. Maybe the art-photo booby pictures are just about his very human insecurities.

Or it could just be me. I've never hobnobbed in Europe—I've never been to Europe; the most international I've ever gone is the Canadian side of Niagara Falls. Maybe I am just a prude, an uptight

American, sexually repressed, opposed to pleasures of the flesh, puritanical, and who am I to judge him? "You can't fault me for my social choices," he told me once. "I'm not breaking any laws. I'm not doing anything illegal or unethical. I'm not doing any harm."

Or maybe it is him, Andrew Boyle. Maybe it has to do with the way Andrew Boyle talks about women, their bodies, their faces, their hair, their clothes. When a woman walks by, he can't not comment on her appearance. He can't not judge her by what would appear to be a very narrow aesthetic. Sometimes his comments remind me of the bitchy things I've heard girls say to each other about other girls. When a blond girl with big breasts and wide hips walked by, he said, "I'm not into dairy princesses."

When a chubby girl wearing too-tight clothes, whose hair was pulled back into a high, tight ponytail, walked by, Andrew said, "That is international, my friends. The white-trash high-and-tight ponytail. You don't just see that in America. I've also seen it in Britain and Spain."

When a skinny brunette with straight hips and perky boobs walked by, and Andrew said, "I'd love for her to model for me," I know there's no way a woman like me can talk to a man like Andrew about another woman's body without having it sound bitchy or insincere or prudish. I don't have to wonder why he's never asked me to model. I know why—I'm too old, too short, too soft—but I don't feel competitive or jealous or worry that my own body doesn't measure up. I stopped worrying about that the day I found a hair growing on my big toe.

The ickiness I feel when I'm around Andrew Boyle and he's looking at women and talking about their bodies is a very old feeling.

It goes back to the morning when I was twelve years old, the morning I woke up with a pair of D-cup breasts and a va-va-voom swing to my walk that horrified my mother and enchanted perverts. As a little girl with enormous boobs, I had a body that attracted attention: from boys my age, of course, who behaved in all the ways one would expect, immaturely and in song, Paul Searle revising the lyrics of the Manhattan Transfer classic "The Boy from New York City" to a version that included my name and the words "has got," "big," and "titty."

It was embarrassing but not nearly as strange and creepy and uncomfortable as the way grown men behaved. Carrie Laughlin's dad circled back around the block to offer me a ride home from school and, in the car, put his arm around me, rubbing my back and squeezing my shoulder. The custodian at John F. Kennedy Junior High suggested I come back to school a little later and "visit" with him awhile. A man older than my dad asked me if I had some milk to go with that shake, did I have a porch to go with that swing. A very old man at the public library asked if I knew where they kept the Louis L'Amour books, then before I could say yes, I know exactly where the westerns are, he kissed me on the mouth, his breath smelling like a cherry cough drop, his tongue tasting like one.

It seemed to me all I was doing was walking down the hall, or down the street, or home from school, or I was looking for a book about magic tricks at the public library, but obviously I was doing something more. I was doing something dirty and wrong. I've never quite gotten over the idea that the body I live in could invite such attention. That something about me—the way I walked, maybe, or the way I chewed gum, the way I dressed, or those really great high-heeled shoes, or that I was such a little girl with such an enormous chest—invited men into thinking it was okay to let me know they wanted something from me, something I didn't want to give them, but since I brought it on myself, maybe I had to.

Do I wear a shirt that's big, bulky, baggy, or do I wear a shirt that clings? Do I hide my body under sweaters and sweatshirts and jackets or do I let the world know I'm female and as a female, I have breasts? Why do I feel so self-conscious anytime I wear a color other than black? Do I want to be looked at or not?

I don't know.

It's me. It's them. It's me. It's Andrew. It's me. It's you. It's any man with greedy eyes. I've never stopped wanting to kick you in the nuts. Hard. When you least expect it.

The Devil I Know
Is the Man Upstairs

My neighbor the Satanist goes up the stairs carrying groceries sacked in paper, not plastic. He comes down the stairs carrying dirty laundry in a wicker basket. He goes up with library books, Blockbuster rentals, a double-dip chocolate chip ice cream cone. He comes down with stacks of neatly bundled newspaper, aluminum cans, and glass bottles, which he loads into the trunk of his car and hauls off to the community recycling center.

The Satanist drives a burgundy 1993 Chevy Lumina. Though the Lumina still has his parents' name on the title, they have all but given it to him. He keeps a red plastic El Diablo bobble head on the dashboard, its black eyebrows high and arched, its teeth white, its lips curled into a devilish smirk. An exotic dancer the Satanist was interested in taking out to the movies turned him down, and the reason she gave was that she didn't care for his El Diablo. She was a Christian girl, she said, and that devil bobble head gave her the creeps.

The Satanist is twenty-six years old. He doesn't smoke. Not cigarettes or cigars or a pipe. Not even marijuana—not even a single tiny hit at a party when everyone else is having some. The Satanist doesn't do drugs. He's never done drugs, doesn't see the point. He'll drink a beer or two—his favorite is Guinness, though Beck's is a close second—but only when he's out somewhere. He doesn't drink to get drunk; he doesn't drink at home; he doesn't drink alone.

Every Sunday, the Satanist calls his parents in Cedarburg, Wisconsin, a suburb of Milwaukee. He asks what's new with them. His mother teaches third grade at a Catholic school, and he likes hearing about the kids in her class, the cute things they say and do. He asks his parents how they're doing, how they're feeling, how's Grandma? The Satanist's grandmother is getting older; her health isn't good, and his father isn't well, either. He has Lou Gehrig's disease, a condition that's almost always fatal. The Satanist can't help but worry about the people he loves. Sometimes he thinks about moving back to Cedarburg, moving back in with his parents so he can be there for his family, so he can be a help.

But other times, he thinks about taking a chance on his dreams. He wrote a screenplay about the mad monk Rasputin and Rasputin's role in the fall of the Romanovs. Sometimes the Satanist dreams about moving to Hollywood, where he would sell his screenplay then make a career out of writing more. Other times, he considers applying to Ph.D. programs so he can work on a degree in film studies.

While he mulls over his next move, the Satanist has a regular weekend gig spinning records at wedding receptions. "People like to do the chicken dance," he tells me. "They like polkas and the hokey-pokey and 'YMCA.' It's irritating, but the Macarena has made a comeback."

The Satanist's mother hasn't exactly been hassling him, but during their Sunday telephone conversations, she's made her wishes clear. She is a practical woman, nice-smelling, more than a few gray hairs, an excellent cook, a devout Catholic, a loving wife and mother. She would like her son to find a job, a good job, one with a 401(k) plan and health insurance that includes eyes and dental. She thinks it's high time he enter the real world.

The Satanist assures her: "Okay, Mom, okay! I'm looking for a job, okay?"

The Satanist wears a shark's tooth on a cord around his neck that he bought at the Minnesota State Fair. He wears baggy jeans and he has a collection of baggy dark T-shirts. One of them has Marilyn Manson on it. Another says 666 in red letters. Another says *Team Satan*, while yet another has a little devil on it and a caption that reads *I'm horny!* One of his T-shirts has a great white shark on it—SHARK ATTACK! it says—and still another has the shark from *Jaws*.

Although he doesn't like getting up early—he's not a morning person—the Satanist likes breakfast food. Juice, toast, potatoes. Bacon and eggs. I've seen him eat a tall stack of pancakes. I've seen him eat a ham and cheese omelet. On Monday, when we went out for breakfast, I didn't ask him if he wanted my home fries, I just said move your toast and I slid them on his plate.

The Satanist is a big-but-not-fat, awkward-moving, sweet-looking guy with a round face, round glasses, and high, thin eyebrows that make him look both skeptical and surprised. He has a nice smile. He has big brown eyes. His hairline is receding. He has pinchable cheeks. I think as raw material, he has potential. He just needs a new wardrobe, better-fitting jeans, and T-shirts that aren't black and faded and advertising things related to sharks or Satan. He needs to trim those fingernails. He definitely needs a better haircut. What he needs is a girlfriend. The love of a good woman is what he needs to forget all about this Satanism business.

Al says it's fine for me to take a Satanist out for breakfast, but what that boy does not need is me meddling in his personal life. "He already has a mother who worries about him," Al says, "and you already have a son. You should worry about your own son."

I point out that my son isn't a Satanist.

"No," Al says, "your son is a thirteen-year-old capitalist."

Al believes the Satanist should be entitled to his own decisions about how he wants to live his life, without interference from me.

"It's not like I'm trying to witness to him. I'm not out to convert him," I say.

"Well, you're no Jerry Falwell," Al says. He squares his fingers like he's a movie director studying me through a camera's lens. "Actually, I see you more as the young Tammy Faye Bakker type."

But maybe I do have a hidden agenda. Maybe these Take a Satanist to Breakfast Mondays are part of my secret mission. I wouldn't dream of offending him, but maybe—because I like the guy; I think he's smart and funny and entertaining and sweet—I don't want him to be a Satanist. Maybe I fret about the condition of his soul and worry over where he's going to spend eternity. Maybe I don't want him to go to hell.

Miss McCade, my childhood Sunday-school teacher, warned me about hell, and if she were here now, she would tell me to watch out! Be on guard! Pray! Because maybe I'm being tested by God. Or maybe I'm being tempted by the devil. You never know what form he may take. Maybe Satan will come knocking on my door claiming he just happened to be in the neighborhood. Maybe he'll tap on my shoulder and ask may I have this dance. He might say smoke this, he might say drink that. He might say take this, it's yours. He could very well call me up and say let's you and me hit the casino. Satan might look me in the eye and tell me breakfast is his favorite meal of the day.

Being friends with a Satanist freaks me out. I can give money to Planned Parenthood, I can wear a T-shirt that says *The Only Bush I Trust Is My Own.* I can support candidates in the Democratic Party and write letters protesting my local government's decision to display an enormous concrete tablet featuring the Ten Commandments in front of the county courthouse. I can offer dollar bills and my cheek to Miss Wile Jane, the ruby-lipped drag queen who has just delighted me with her lip-synched performance of "Redneck Woman." I can conjure up all sorts of wildness, all kinds of wickedness, a variety of wantonness, but ask one little Satanist does he like grape jelly on his toast and I'm hearing Miss McCade's voice in my head. She's whispering, *Girl, you are on the highway to hell.*

Al doesn't have a Miss McCade in his past, but that's because he was a Unitarian. That was a long time ago, and only for a short while, and only because there were cute little hippie girls at the Unitarian Universalist Church. Al remembers these girls fondly. They loved Jesus and they were real wild. Al says they prayed for him, but they also turned him on to some good drugs. He says he dropped mescaline in that church once, courtesy of the hippie girls. He also says those Unitarian hippie girls were loose.

"Another plus in my book," he says.

Even though that particular church had a lot to offer, once Al returned home from Vietnam, he put religion forever behind him like it was an incredibly hard test he crammed for, only to pass and forget about. He survived a war, and rather than thanking God for getting him through it, he questioned why any God who loved him would send him to Southeast Asia in the first place. Thus, Al has no interest in or tolerance for religious concerns, my own or anyone else's. I can't even get him to go to Christmas Vespers to hear the choir.

But I've always had a religious streak. When I was little and someone asked me what I wanted to be when I grew up, I said a Catholic. It seemed like the easy religion, and the most fun. I envied the Catholic kids at school. Their CCD classes. Their Christmas Midnight Mass. Their accessories: rosaries, medallions, candles, a Saint Francis birdbath for the garden, a plastic Jesus for the dashboard of your car. I liked how Catholics played bingo— with cigarettes and daubers, with gusto and nuns. Their weddings lasted for hours and were followed by spaghetti dinner receptions at the town fire hall. It seemed to me that, unlike people from my church, Catholics knew how to throw a party, knew how to worship God and still have a pretty good time. I wanted to wear a lacy white First Holy Communion dress. I wanted to pick a confirmation name. I wanted a party, a sheet cake, and a kindhearted priest who'd act as mediator between me and God, the way my mother did when she was breaking it to my father that I'd gotten another bad grade in math. I wanted a religion where followers didn't seem so fixated on where they'd spend the afterlife and knew where I could buy a raffle ticket that might win me a thousand bucks at the Saint Vitus Bazaar.

People from my church said Catholics aren't true Christians. In fact, people from my church said Catholics are misled, misguided, just flat-out wrong. Satan has tricked them, and because of their willful blindness, Catholics are going to hell.

It's partly because Catholics gamble and worship false idols like the Virgin Mary and all those weird saints, and what is with that hocus-pocus jibber-jabber to Saint What's-his-face they run in the classified ads?

It's partly because Catholics don't read the Bible. Some of them don't even have a Bible. How can they ever know the Word of God if they don't read the Bible?

But the big deal breaker, what truly keeps Catholics locked outside the gates of heaven no matter how good they've been, no matter how much good they've done—and, Mother Teresa, this includes you!—is that they have not accepted Jesus Christ as their personal savior. They haven't invited Jesus into their hearts. It's a real Christian's moral obligation to explain to them that this is the wrong road. That this is the one true highway to hell.

Jewish people are going to hell. Muslims, too. So are Mormons and Christian Scientists, Jehovah's Witnesses and Unitarian hippie chicks. So are Hindus and Buddhists and Rastafarians, queers and lesbians, feminists and communists, Quakers and Mennonites, Democrats, and all the Baldwin brothers except Stephen (he went born-again after 9/11). So are the native peoples in places like the Congo and the Dominican Republic and the Ivory Coast.

Satanists are most definitely going to hell.

So are you.

Unless you accept Jesus Christ as your personal savior. Unless you welcome Him into your heart.

Which I have.

More than once.

I went to church every Sunday morning when I was growing up. My mother woke me, then my two brothers. She poured us bowls of cereal or fried us some eggs. She made sure we were nicely dressed, our faces washed, our teeth brushed, our cowlicks slicked down. Then she sent us off to church with my aunt and her family, kindly people who agreed to assume responsibility for our souls on Sundays between eight-thirty and noon.

"Bye-bye, kids," my mother would say.

Sometimes, when we got home, there would be a box of Dunkin' Donuts on the kitchen counter or the house would smell like bacon. Sometimes, my parents' bed wasn't made. Sometimes, my mother would be singing and my father would be taking a nap. As far as my parents were concerned, they'd come into a win-win situation: they had the house completely to themselves for several hours, their children were learning about God from experts, and this babysitting/moral instruction didn't cost them a dime.

The Christian and Missionary Alliance church my brothers and I attended had two items on its eternal to-do list:

(1) Send Christian and Missionary Alliance missionaries to places like the Congo, the Dominican Republic, and the Ivory Coast to spread the Good News about Jesus; build Christian and Missionary Alliance churches; and convert the natives.

(2) Prepare for the Second Coming.

Item Number One didn't seem so bad to me. The first Sunday of every month was Missionary Sunday, which meant a slide show that included photographs of mud huts and scrawny donkeys and women lugging jugs of water on top of their heads. At the beginning of the slide show, we saw pictures of skinny, barefooted, sad-eyed, dark-skinned children wearing skirts made of twigs and leaves. By the end of the show, these same kids had fattened up. They were wearing our surplus tie-dyed Vacation Bible School T-shirts from the summer of 1981. They were wearing Easter shoes we'd outgrown. They were holding Bibles. Those kids were grinning ear-to-ear, and they were giving a thumbs-up. They were finally happy and at peace and well fed. When they died, those kids would go to heaven. Because they knew Jesus.

Item Number Two, however, preparing for the Second Coming, gave me nightmares worse than the flying-monkey-from-The-Wizard-of-Oz bad dreams, worse than dreams of falling out of the sky, worse than the dream where I'm at the National Spelling Bee, naked and unable to spell *formaldehyde* in front of my teachers and family and peers, and infinitely worse than the dream where Miss McCade stands before our Sunday-school class and explains what Bob Seger meant when he said he was working on his night moves.

Miss McCade was a sweet old lady whose panty hose wrinkled some around her knees and her ankles. She had tightly permed gray hair, and every week she wore the same lavender-gray skirt and jacket. It would take me years to identify that she smelled like old lady: rose-scented lotion and Ben-Gay. It was Miss McCade's job, her calling, to prepare children between the ages of twelve and seventeen for the Second Coming.

Preparing for the Second Coming means you have to be on call at all times, always on your best behavior. Because as it says in Matthew 24:36, "of that day and hour knoweth no man," and since the Second Coming, also known as the Rapture, can happen at any time, it would not do to be caught in a compromising position. It would not do to be fornicating on the Day of Rapture, for example, or sitting alone in your bedroom spilling your seed, or even merely considering the secrets of what is under clothing, your own or anyone else's. It would not do to be caught swaying while flicking a Bic lighter at a Bob Seger or Black Sabbath concert. It wouldn't do to even be listening to Seger or Sabbath on vinyl, eight-track, or cassette tape.

Don't you know the letters in KISS stand for Kids in Satan's Service? Miss McCade would say. AC/DC means After Christ, the Devil Comes. And don't even think about listening to that especially beguiling music known as Christian Rock. There is no Christian Rock. That's just another one of Satan's tricks designed to distract you from knowing the Lord, Miss McCade would say.

Every Sunday she'd remind us that we needed to stay on our toes because no man knoweth the day and hour. She'd say, "I sure wouldn't want to be sitting in a movie theater when Jesus comes." She'd say, "I sure wouldn't want to be playing poker when Jesus comes." She'd say, "I sure wouldn't want to be drunk on beer when Jesus comes."

Sometimes, during Sunday services, listening to the preacher call forth anyone who wanted a fresh start, anyone who accepted Christ's redemption, anyone who needed God's forgiveness, I'd feel such loneliness and longing that I went forth to be saved, and I even said I was saved: I announced it, proclaimed it, declared it, but really, I never felt like it took. I never felt differently from how I did before. I wanted to believe, but I second-guessed my motives.

It wasn't Jesus' voice telling me to cover my ears when I walked past the duplex where the guitar-playing hippies lived and I heard them singing *I set out running but I take my time, a friend of the devil is a friend of mine*, it was Miss McCade's. Miss McCade's was the voice in my head when, annoyed with my mother, I purposely stepped on a crack in the sidewalk. *I sure wouldn't want to be breaking my mother's back when Jesus comes.*

For years and years, Miss McCade had the power to mess with my head. Fears about what I would and wouldn't want to be doing when Jesus came screwed up a lot of otherwise perfectly fun Friday nights at frat parties or keggers or in the backseats of cars.

Miss McCade's voice wormed through my thoughts especially insistently when I'd been smoking marijuana. *I sure wouldn't want to be doped up on Thai stick when Jesus comes*, Miss McCade would say, mocking me, and she tugged on the ends of her perm. One time, during a party at the Theta Xi house, Miss McCade hitched up her saggy panty hose, then turned to me and quoted from Hebrews 10:26–27: "For if we sin wilfully after we have received the knowledge of the truth, there remaineth no sacrifice for sins, but a certain fearful looking for of judgment and fiery indignation, which shall devour the adversaries."

"Will somebody please please please make that chick shut the fuck up about raging hellfire?" a frat boy said. "Because the way she's going on about it is really stomping on my buzz."

When I was in fifth grade, at Vacation Bible School, there was a contest for memorizing Bible verses. The prize was a globe with brown crosses on all the countries where missionaries were bringing the Word to the natives and the natives to the Light. I was determined to win. The lazy kids all memorized "Jesus wept," while smart-asses liked stuff from Leviticus—Leviticus 18:23, for example: "Neither shalt thou lie with any beast to defile thyself therewith: neither shall any woman stand before a beast to lie down thereto: it is confusion"—but I was obsessed with the verses that describe hell.

I still have a great imagination for the place. Hell is as far from heaven as you can get. The people there are cackling and crackling, flailing and wailing, weeping and gnashing their teeth. The image of weeping and gnashing of teeth is referenced in the Bible in seven different verses (six in the Book of Matthew; one in Luke), and at age eleven, I could recite every one of them.

Twenty-five years later, I can't recite the exact words to those seven verses well enough to win another contest, but the feeling they gave me has never left. It's a creepy, jittery feeling, but it's also enticing, like peeking at a scary movie through your fingers. Sometimes, in the mornings when I wake up, my jaw is clenched and aching, my head is pounding, I feel like my teeth are chipped, broken, in shards.

Al tells me I need to chill out. Because what if there's another possibility? What if when you die, that's it, that's the end, there is no God, no heaven, no eternal damnation, no fiery pit, no Miss McCade? What if there's just nothingness. Al says that's what he believes, so why not be a nice person but still have a good time.

When I was in college, I read *Pensées*, a work by a seventeenth-century French philosopher, Blaise Pascal, who encouraged me to put my money on God. Might as well, Pascal said. If you believe, and He exists, the payoff is huge. But if you don't believe, and God is real, you're screwed. If you believe, and it turns out there is no God, then really, what have you lost? Pascal believed people were lousy anyway—"How hollow is the heart of man," he wrote in *Pensées*, "and how full of excrement!"—so why not live a virtuous life? Why not believe, and live like you believe, and maybe, just maybe, you'll end up behaving your way to belief?

Pascal sounds a lot like Dr. Phil, who says you can behave your way to success, and Pascal also reminds me a lot of my father, who said I do as I'm told because if I didn't there'd be hell to pay.

Something in me resisted my father; it's the same something that thinks it's Dr. Phil who is full of excrement. Maybe it's the desire to live a fiery and interesting life, a longing for adventure. Maybe it's that I have an appreciation for fornication, intoxication, and AC/DC. Maybe it's that I think Saturday night is more fun than Sunday morning, and if Eve didn't pick that apple, there'd be no apple pie.

Al says he's going to turn his beliefs into his own religion, his own church; he can make good use out of the nonprofit tax status. He says he'll be the spiritual leader of this new faith—no, actually, he will be God—and it will be my job to secure the compound, bring him virgins, and hang out at airports selling roses. He says he's putting my friend the Satanist in charge of making sure there are enough clean flowing white robes for everyone. He says his new religion is going to combine the pacifist teachings of Buddha with the doll-making practices of voodoo. "I'm going to call it Boo-Doo," Al says. "At the beginning of services, my members will chant 'Who do Boo-Doo? We do and you do!' five times. Then we'll drink some beer, play some poker, and have some laughs. Then church is over. Until next time."

I laugh, but secretly, part of me is nervous. Part of me is pretty certain that God in heaven—and certainly Miss McCade—is annoyed at Al but that they're saving their real wrath for me. Because I laugh at blasphemy instead of setting the blasphemer straight. Because I haven't brought the Satanist to the Lord. Because I was raised in the Christian and Missionary Alliance church, and that means I've been told, I should know, I've been given the truth and made aware of the consequences, so what part of eternal damnation do I not understand? Miss McCade pats me on the hand, saying, *Girl, it's going to be hot where you're going.*

The Girl Who Only
Sometimes Said No

Yesterday my son was turning the pages in his eighth-grade yearbook so we could play a game I came up with called Guess Which Kids Are Retarded. The boy thought the game was terrible, so cruel and so mean that I should have to pay a fine, I should have to pay him ten bucks every time I was wrong.

But I refused to pay him anything. I was horrible at guessing who was and who wasn't retarded. I've never been good at knowing something about a person just by looking at him. The ones I thought were special needs for sure turned out to be some of the coolest kids in the class, and the ones who actually were mentally retarded looked to me like members of the chess club. The problem, I decided, is that most human beings between the ages of twelve and fifteen look like their needs are special. Their necks are too skinny to hold up their heads. Their teeth are shiny and enormous. There is a shifty, furtive look in their eyes, and their tongues frequently stick out at odd angles.

All the girls who I thought were sort of cute my son said yuck about. The girl he pointed out as hot did not looked retarded. She looked pleased to be in front of a camera. She looked like typical cheerleader material, all blond and blue-eyed, skinny and pretty and prissy. Then he pointed to a different girl. He informed me that this girl is a slut.

"A slut?" I said. "She's thirteen years old! How can she be a slut? You don't even know what a slut is. What does that word mean to you, 'slut'? I mean, how are you defining your term? You can't just call a girl a slut and not explain what you mean by it."

The boy rolled his eyes. "What I mean," he said with exaggerated patience, "is she's been with too many guys."

"Too many guys!" I said. "Too many guys!"

The boy wanted to know why was I so worked up.

When I asked him how many guys are too many guys, he said it wasn't something that could be pinned down to a specific number. When I asked him what do you mean by "been with," what do you think "been with" implies, he said it could mean a lot of things, none of which he cared to discuss with his mother. When I asked him, well, then, how could you possibly know this girl is a slut, what evidence do you have, he said he didn't have any evidence. He said he didn't need any. He just knew.

"Right," I said. "It's one of those things a person just knows. Yes. Right. Of course. It's instinctual."

Because the boy spent most of his free time burrowed up in his room, playing endless hours of Halo, slack-jawed and mouth-breathing, pale and getting paler, hopped up on Red Bull and Oreos, pepperoni pizza and Doritos, his eyes glazed over, his breath bad, his legs atrophied from lack of use, I figured he didn't have any biblical knowledge of this girl's sluttiness. It just wasn't possible. One would have to leave his room for that to happen. One would need to take a shower every now and then. One would have to put down his joystick.

"It's not a joystick!" he shouted. "I keep telling you that! It's a controller, okay?"

I studied the slut's yearbook picture. Long dark hair. Brown eyes. Her neck was scrawny. She was smiling and her teeth looked really big. She looked like everyone else. Unless there was someone in the know available to point it out, you'd never guess this girl was a slut. She looked like a regular thirteen-year-old girl.

Maybe it was in how she dressed. I asked the boy if this girl dressed like a slut.

"When I was her age," I told him, "I had a belt buckle that said *Boy Toy*. As soon as I walked out of the house, I went in the alley and rolled up the waistband on my skirt. I once wore my father's blue cardigan sweater to school. As a *dress*." I paused, raising my eyebrows so he'd understand I meant business. "It was all I wore."

The boy said what he didn't understand was why I was making such a big deal about this. "I mean, what is your problem?" he said.

"That's for me to know and you to find out," I told him. I asked my son is this girl the slut of the whole class, the slut of the whole eighth grade.

He said she was.

"Well, then," I said, "you need to know there are worse things a girl can be. She could be a person who tortures small animals, for example, or she could be someone who eats paste. She could be the girl who wears white shoes after Labor Day. White shoes after

Labor Day!" I said. "That's a crime about a thousand times worse than being an eighth-grade slut."

I could tell the boy wanted to argue that nobody eats paste in eighth grade, not even the retarded kids, and lots of people wear white shoes year-round. He'd go on about white Reeboks, white Nikes, white Adidas—he was so predictable! But I'd already closed the yearbook. I told him Guess Which Kids Are Retarded was a terrible game, a mean game, and that I didn't want to ever hear him refer to a girl as a slut again, that girl or any other. As far as I was concerned, the matter was resolved.

"Fine," he said. "She's not a slut."

"I'm pleased to hear you say that."

The boy paused.

"She's a skanky ho bag."

In that moment, and for the rest of the day, I hated boys, just hated them.

I haven't always hated boys. There have been times when I liked them quite a bit.

I was the girl who liked boys so much that she kissed them on the first date. Sometimes I did even more. I once watched a shirtless boy, his body lean and tan, his stomach flat and muscled, his T-shirt hanging out of the back pocket of his jeans, show off for me. He did crunches while hanging upside down from the monkey bars at Lincoln Park—*ninety-six, ninety-seven, ninety-eight*—and when he got to one hundred, I applauded. Then I took off my shirt.

I was a girl who'd take off her shirt herself, reaching one-handed behind her back to spring open her bra. I left my footprint on the passenger's side window of a car. The guy and I got busted that night, twice, by the same cop, a bulky, jug-eared man named Officer McCormick who suggested the first time that we get on down the road. The second time he rubbed his eyes, said he had a headache, told us he had three young daughters at home who he hated to think might someday be pawed at in a car. He looked at me, sadly, it seemed, and said, "Miss, why don't you ask your gentleman friend to take you on home. It would be the honorable thing for him to do."

But the minute Officer McCormick turned his back, my gentleman friend called me Scarlett O'Hara and I called him Rhett Butler, and we giggled and talked dirty about my honor in southern accents until one of us—okay, it was me—suggested the lake is a good place to park.

So I did slutty things. Maybe I was even sort of a slut. I probably was a slut. There were boys and other girls who thought so, said so, told each other so.

My son doesn't know this about me. He would probably be humiliated, demoralized, shocked. He'd probably consider it a form of child abuse if I ever revealed that I once had car sex with this guy on the first date, and then afterward, I opened the door and puked up a very expensive bottle of red wine. "The guy was your father, dude!" I could tell him. "What do you think of them apples?" I could say, and "Who are you calling a slut now?"

My son would be mortified, scandalized, pained to learn his mother was a girl who carried condoms in her purse or in her pocket. I kept a box of condoms in the nightstand next to my bed.

The boy doesn't know that, but he does know about condoms. When he was five years old, he walked up to me in Rite Aid carrying a big handful, about twenty condoms individually wrapped in shiny gold foil. They kept falling out of his hands. He wanted to know what are these and what are they for.

I know he wanted them to be candy, like those chocolate coins he'd get in his Christmas stocking. "Those are condoms," I told him. "A man wears one when he doesn't want to make a baby."

"Oh, condoms," the boy said, like it was a word he'd known but forgotten, like oh, of course, condoms.

"Hmmmmmp," the boy said, as in I'll-be-darned and How-about-that. "Do I need one?" he wanted to know.

I told him he'd always need one. I told him sex is fun, especially when you're young and strong and healthy, and you like living in your body, but you always, always wear a condom.

"Should I put one on right now?" he said.

After I got the boy home from Rite Aid, I gave him the big talk. I thought I did a pretty good job. I wasn't squeamish or shy or embarrassed as I told him everything I could think of concerning sex. I was frank and up-front and honest, and I did not use ridiculous words like "winky-dinky" or "willy" or "pecker" or "coochie." I called the parts of the body by their proper names, I said "penis" and "vagina," "testicles" and "secondary sex organs," I explained what various acts are and how they are performed, I talked about how some boys like girls and some boys like boys, and that's okay. "Do you think you like boys or girls?" I asked him.

"Girls stink," he said, "but I'll marry one anyway."

I showed the boy my copy of *Our Bodies, Ourselves*, I translated slang, I told him about masturbation. I wanted to cover everything.

"Hmmmmmmp," the boy would occasionally say, as in That's-really-something, as in Imagine-that and Whodda-thunk-it?

Finally, I asked him if he had any questions.

"Can I go to the bathroom?" he said.

"Hurry!" I said. "Come right back! There's still more!"

But when half an hour passed, and he didn't come back, I went looking for him. I found him cross-legged on the floor in his bedroom, playing with Legos. He was listening to his Barney CD, something he hadn't done since he turned five and declared he'd had enough, he was never watching children's programming on public television ever again.

I asked him did he have any questions about what we'd just been talking about? Did he have any questions about sex?

He said yes.

"Ask me anything!" I said brightly. "Anything!"

He said, "What would have happened if you were a person, and Dad was an eagle, and you guys had sex, and there was an egg, a gigantic egg, and when it hatched, a baby came out, and the baby was me. Would I have a beak? Would I have talons? Would I be able to fly? It would be cool if I was half a human and half a predator bird."

"Wait right here," I told him, and I pulled my copy of *Bulfinch's Mythology* off the shelf and opened it to Leda and the Swan. While he played with Legos, I told him the story of Zeus in the form of a long-necked bird raping the beautiful Leda. I fully intended to use this as a launching point for talking about sex that's consensual and sex that's not consensual, but something in the boy's face stopped me. I think he was imagining himself emerging from a cracked egg, complete with wings, talons, a beak. I think he was imagining himself flying high above the earth, swooping down to spear a fish or a rabbit, then swooping back up to the tallest tree.

"Hmmmmmp," the boy was saying, shaking his head, as in Wouldn't-that-just-take-the-cake, as in Wouldn't-that-just-be-the-greatest-thing-ever.

I didn't stop talking to the boy about sex. Every so often, something would inspire me—the banana I was about to slice over his Cheerios, say, or the cigar the old man at the bus stop was chewing on, or the tubelike water balloon he was itchy to throw at me—and I'd point at the boy, I'd remind him, "You always wear a condom! Do you hear me? You always wear a condom!"

As the boy got older, he grew sick of hearing about it. "I know! I know!" he'd say. "You don't have to keep telling me that."

"You're torturing him," my friend Steven told me. "Ten years from now, when he's finally having sex, he's going to hear his mother's voice in his head. And that's not something any guy wants to hear." Steven looked mournful. He was thirty-four years old and spoke to his mother every morning at seven o'clock; if he didn't call her at seven, she called him at seven-oh-five. Steven patted my hand, saying, "It's not good for a guy to learn about sex from his mother. Let him learn from his friends. That's how I learned, and that's where my son will learn. It really is the best way."

When my son came home from the sex ed talk he received in fifth grade, I asked him how it went. I was feeling pretty smug, pretty satisfied with my parenting skills, but the boy was furious with me. He said, "You said you told me everything! You did not tell me everything!"

Apparently, I'd neglected to tell him about his vas deferens, a part of the male anatomy I'd never given much thought to. In fact, I wasn't even sure where it was or what it was for. Later that night, after the boy had gone to bed, I'd look *vas deferens* up on WebMD.com.

But right now, I was playing it cool. "Vas deferens?" I said. "Oh, yes. That's the German rock band, right?"

The boy did not find me amusing.

"A Swedish pastry chef?"

He glared, and I couldn't help myself, I said it: "Between men and women, there is a vas deferens."

The boy said if that was supposed to be a joke, he didn't get it, and I told him you will someday. I have always hated the You-will-someday response. It's another way adults can say I know something you don't know, but it's also a way adults can avoid discussing matters for which they have no answers.

I t was easier to talk to my son when he was too young to do anything with the information. Now that he's older, it's more worrisome. I've been trying to think of what I could say to the boy about sex that I haven't already said. If he feels like he's justified to call a girl a slut, then I feel like I've done something wrong, like I haven't said the right thing, I haven't said enough, like I've somehow done him a wrong. I've talked plenty about penises and vaginas but maybe I haven't talked enough about the heart. Maybe I haven't said enough how easy it is to confuse love with lust, loneliness with longing. Maybe I need to say something about how important it is to be kind and careful with someone else's heart.

I was younger than my son is right now the first time I got my heart broken. I got my first kiss from Mickey Galileo, who claimed he was a direct descendant of the Italian astronomer who invented the telescope and studied the stars. For a twelve-year-old's pick-up line, it wasn't so bad. In fact, it must have had its charm, because Mickey Galileo planted first kisses on all the girls in my neighborhood.

During our senior year of high school, Mickey would mullet his hair, and then he would perm his mullet, but now it flopped flat in a long shaggy cap over his head. I didn't like Mickey's hair, or the way he stared at my chest, or how he ran his hand up and down my back to feel if I was wearing a bra, but I did like when he pressed his chap-lipped mouth against mine, and because I liked it, I really liked it, I thought I really liked Mickey Galileo. I thought I might even love him. When Mickey told me he needed his mom's gold bracelet back because he didn't like me anymore, he was Brenda Tucci's boyfriend now, I cried. I was sad because Mickey didn't love me, but what really got me down was that without Mickey, there would be no more kissing. There was no one else for me to kiss.

But then, one day after school, Nathan Evans and I stood in my backyard, and while Nella and Duchess and Schmitty, our family mongrels, wagged their tails and watched, Nathan pushed me up against the steel-gray siding of my house so he could uncurl his tongue in my mouth. Nathan was not particularly good-looking. His eyelashes and eyebrows were so pale he might as well not have had any at all. His face was long and narrow. His teeth were humongous, and his neck was skinny except for his Adam's apple.

Only, I didn't care how he looked. I only cared about the kissing, how it made me feel a feeling that at the time seemed indescribable, though I would now identify that feeling as horny. Very horny. I was thirteen years old.

I thought I was in love with Nathan Evans. I imagined we'd get married so we could kiss like this every day, but I'd have to adopt children since I wouldn't want any kid of mine to inherit those icky invisible eyebrows. As his mouth slurped and sucked at mine, I tried it out, those words. I murmured, "I love you, Nathan Evans." We kissed and kissed. We kissed from three-thirty to five, which was when Nella and Duchess and Schmitty started barking for their supper. Once their barking turned into howling, my mother hollered for me to feed them, and Nathan Evans, whose lips were red and puffy and swollen from all that kissing, rode away on his bike. I'd never been so happy.

Until the next day at school.

There was noise rising out of the hallways at John F. Kennedy Junior High School, and there was noise rolling out of the lunchroom and slamming off the walls in the gym, the library, my homeroom, my math class, English, social studies, home ec, and everywhere else in the school. The noise was loud and it got louder, and it all seemed to be about me. How I had sex with Nathan Evans. How I fucked him right there in my parents' backyard.

Bruce Carleton, a boy I'd known since kindergarten, licked his tongue across his lips when I passed him in the hall. Jonas Jones stuck his tongue out and wagged it at me. During lunch, Raymond Dantico kept his tongue in his mouth, but thrust it against his cheek while making throaty little moans. Billy Argot and Mark Haven and William Wikiera moaned and grunted, while Freddie Stone asked me did it hurt.

All day that day, I kept it together. I was humiliated, I was heartbroken, but I kept my head up, I didn't cry. While I was putting forth the notion that the very idea of Nathan Evans made me want to vomit, Nathan Evans was avoiding me, going out of his way not to look at me. As far as he was concerned, his work was done. In the eyes of his peers, he'd become a man, while I became a slut. A tramp. A whore. A Girl with a Bad Reputation.

I think back to that day, and there he is, I see him, the boy. Not Nathan Evans, or Freddie Stone, or Bruce Carleton, but the only boy who matters. My son. I see him wandering through the hallways of John F. Kennedy Junior High with the rest of them. He's wearing jeans and a white T-shirt, and a Penn State hat even though it's against the rules to wear a baseball cap in the school. He's chewing on a toothpick. He's slouching against the lockers. He's admiring his biceps. He's as arrogant as only a thirteen-year-old boy can be. He's sure of himself and his place in the world, just as he's sure that girl walking by is a slut. Hey, he shouts at her. Hey! Did you remember to use a condom? Well? Did you?

There are still other things I could tell the boy.

At age sixteen, during the National Academic Games Tournament, I lost my virginity to a boy named Keith from the New Orleans team: something about that Louisiana accent, something about the way he called me honey like he was a grown man and I was a small child. He's a doctor now.

When I was seventeen, I dated a guy named Pete who was majoring in physical education at Youngstown State University. Every Friday night, he took me to a movie, he bought me an ice cream cone, he made out with me in his basement, he took me home in time for my curfew. It never went any further than that. He said he respected me too much to have sex with me, though I didn't see what respect had to do with my pounding heart, my hot skin. Years later, I ran into his best friend, Ed, at a Rolling Stones concert. Ed informed me that after Pete took me home, he went to a strip club, he spent his student loan money on lap dances. Pete is a fireman now, and I wonder does he know that after the Stones concert, I made out with his best friend, Ed, out of spite and years too late, payback for all those lap dances.

At eighteen, I was crazy about a philosophy major named Rick, who was long and lean, black-haired and green-eyed, whom I let condescend to me just because I liked the way he looked. He's the unemployed father of daughters now, but back then he was so smooth.

I could tell my son that I said yes a lot, but I did sometimes say no. I did!

I said no to a guy named Jimmy who asked me out during a parenting class. Such a class was required by the State of Colorado when a divorcing couple has a minor child. Jimmy was fat. Hairy. Wearing a thick gold chain. He wanted to know would I like to go out dancing with him after parenting class?

I said no to the boy who asked me out while standing in line at McDonald's. This was, of course, when I still ate at McDonald's, before I saw *Super Size Me*, when I was still greedy for a McDonald's cheeseburger and chocolate shake. I was twenty-eight years old, my would-be suitor was maybe sixteen.

I don't know what I said to Billy Zeigler, a boy I knew in college. I don't know what I did with Billy Zeigler. I don't know what happened that night except that I drank a lot, too much, I passed out, and when I woke up, blurry and stiff, sticky and fuzzy-headed, Billy Zeigler informed me it wasn't rape, he did not rape me. "You better never say I raped you," he said, "because I didn't." Then he said here's your coat, I'll walk you to your dorm.

I try not to think about that night, what may or may not have happened.

There are still other things I could tell him, the boy, my son.

Things like:

If I had fucked Nathan Evans, then you'd have no eyebrows! The point is, if a girl's been nice enough to let you touch her boob, the respectful thing to do is keep it to yourself.

And:

Though your father and I did have sex in the car on the first date, and I did throw up afterward, he was really sweet about it, holding back my hair and offering to buy me some 7Up. Of course, none of this is why we got a divorce.

And:

It really is very simple. When a girl is too drunk to know she's having sex, one should not have sex with her.

And:

I liked falling in love with boys. I fell in love easily, happily, a lot. I fell in love with gay boys and bad boys, boys I'd met at the bar, frat boys, and the boy my college roommate liked. From the age of thirteen to the present, I have fallen in love with a red-headed paraplegic and a balding mathematician and the French student who bagged my groceries. I fell in love with a logger, a poet, a colleague. I was smitten with the doctor who delivered my son, I had a crush on an arrogant dark-haired musician with a trust fund,

I was so wildly infatuated with a potter who had big hands and long fingers that in an attempt to show him how desirable and fun and sexy I was, I came on to his friend the filmmaker right in front of him. Two days later, when the filmmaker invited me to go away for a weekend, I didn't go.

See? I could say. Sometimes I really did say no!

But only sometimes, the boy might point out. There were still a lot of guys. There's no denying you've been with a lot of guys.

I could ask him if he thinks "a lot" means the same as "too many." I could prepare myself for his answer. I could try to change his mind about sluts, like me, like the girl in his eighth-grade year-book, like so many girls he's yet to meet. I could tell him that he shouldn't call a girl a slut because someday she might be somebody's mother. I could tell him maybe she's a slut because she's lonely, she's sad, she's hoping someone or something will make the lonely and sad go away.

It won't, of course. It never does. But nonetheless, there's not a girl who's more hopeful than a slut, more optimistic. She may give in but she doesn't give up. She keeps looking, she keeps hoping, she's always waiting for that someone who will say it: I love you, too.

Lighten Up

It was love-hate. It was passive-aggressive, it was self-destructive and unnecessarily complicated, and I cared what he thought of me way too much and for much too long.

And he wasn't even my father or someone I was sleeping with.

The first time I saw Gerry Hawthorne, he was standing outside Wilkinson Hall, smoking a cigarette. I was newly hired to teach two sections of freshmen composition at the same state college where Gerry was the English department chair. He was wearing shorts and sandals and a purple T-shirt with a pocket that contained a pack of Camels. Because he was my boss, I thought he'd be an important person to make nice to, especially since I wanted to someday go from teaching part-time to teaching full-time, and he seemed approachable, easygoing, fun. I was certain I'd like him.

Mostly, it was the Camels that gave me this impression. I was a smoker, too, and because I had no reason to believe otherwise, I thought all people who smoked were cool.

DIANA JOSEPH

At this time, smokers were relegated to smoking outside. We grumbled about it, of course, especially if it was rainy or windy, too hot or too cold—smokers prefer to smoke in comfort—but rough weather should never quell the desire to light up. If it does, you are but a dabbler, a poser, an I-only-smoke-when-I'm-drinking-can-I-bum-one dilettante. You are a phony.

I took up smoking at age fourteen: my father's unfiltered Lucky Strikes, my uncle's Winstons, whatever long butts I found in the gutter or scored out of public ashtrays. In high school, I puffed on Capris. You are what you smoke, my friends and I told one another, and these were cigarettes as feminine and elegant, as long and slender, as every girl wished she could be. In college, when I smoked Camels, it was because I was strong and independent, bold. When I switched to mentholated cigarettes—Marlboro Greens, Kools, Salems—it was because I had a head cold or strep throat. Before long, I was smoking menthol all the time.

I liked being a girl who smoked, but even more than that, I liked drawing smoke into my lungs then exhaling. I liked smoking. I thought it made me look mysterious, I loved how it looked in photographs. I was grateful for the reason smoking gave me to take a break from the task at hand and loiter in front of buildings. Smoking was a way to pass the time. It was something to do with my hands. It was the pleasure that came after finishing a meal, or while driving, or talking on the telephone, or sipping morning coffee. Smoking was also a way to socialize, to bond, to connect, a perfectly good excuse to stand beside my department chair and speak to him, to introduce myself then say, do you have a light? Which he did.

Twenty minutes later, Gerry and I were downtown, walking

into a bar. Three hours later, after I'd smoked all my cigarettes and he was blitzed on bourbon, he patted my hand, my hair, and told me I was very nice, he was very glad to have me in the department, would I please give him a ride home?

A s chair of my department, Gerry Hawthorne could determine how comfortable or uncomfortable my life would be. He decided how many classes I taught, what those classes were, and the day and time I taught them.

He'd swing by my office a couple of times a day to invite me to step outside, where we talked about literature or teaching or students over a cigarette or two or three. That was when I admired him the most, those times when he'd let me feel dazzled by his insight, respectful of his smarts. When he was Dr. Gerald Hawthorne, Ph.D. When we were on campus, I asked his advice about literature or teaching or students. I went to him with questions, problems, concerns. I listened when he talked about Gertrude Stein, how she and Hemingway had been great friends, how she helped Hemingway become a great writer, and how, when their friendship ended, Hemingway changed her famous "Rose is a rose is a rose" to "Bitch is a bitch is a bitch."

"Hemingway was cool, man," Gerry said.

But off campus, on Friday afternoons, Gerry Hawthorne drank beer. Then he downed a shot or two of bourbon. He smoked a bunch of cigarettes, then he drank more beer. Sometimes when he'd been drinking at someone's house, he reached the point where he wanted to crank up some tunes—the sound track to *Jesus Christ Superstar* was a favorite, though he also liked *Abbey*

Road, *Tommy*, and early Kinks—and he instructed us to push all the living room furniture out of the way so he could dance. Gerry Hawthorne was in his young forties, a clumsy guy, inelegantly constructed, a flat butt, skinny legs, and a stomach that meant business, that gave him size and bulk and allowed him to bully his way through a crowd. When Gerry danced, which was only if he'd been drinking, he hopped on one leg while raising the other stiffly in front of him, like he was doing the monster mash. He held a cigarette in one hand and he held the other hand straight out, optimistic that this positioning would keep him balanced and upright. When Gerry Hawthorne danced, he had a very good time.

Sometimes drinking made Gerry feel affectionate toward others. It made him feel like giving out compliments. *Shhhhh! Don't tell anyone*, he might breathe hotly in your ear, *but you're so very beautiful! I have always had a secret crush on you!* Though he was married—Gerry had been married to his childhood sweetheart for over twenty years—murmuring such sweet nothings always made him feel like smooching. He did not discriminate. Man or woman, married or single, homely or attractive, Gerry Hawthorne would lean forward, pucker up, and plant a big kiss right on your mouth. His kisses were slobbery, his kisses tasted like beer, his breath smelled like cigarettes, his beard and moustache tickled. He'd stroke your hand, smiling fondly at you, saying, *You're so nice, you're my friend, I like you.*

This was when I adored him the most, these times when I thought he had more personality than ten people, and was more fun than twenty. Oftentimes, Gerry wanted someone who had a guitar to get out that guitar and strum some chords so he could make up a song. One of his best compositions was called "Take Me

Downtown, Dante." It was a musical plea for our friend Dante to drive Gerry to the bars downtown so he could drink some more. *Take me downtown, Dante,* he spoke-sang in a voice that was plain-tive and bluesy, a scratchy voice that made one think of hound dogs and heartbreak and pulled-pork barbecue sandwiches. *Take me downtown, please! Take me downtown, Dante! I know you got the keys!*

I don't remember if Dante took Gerry downtown that day, but there were occasions when I took Gerry to a bar downtown. There were times when I took Gerry to the liquor store to buy more bour-bon. If the phone rang, and it was after last call, I got out of bed to pick Gerry up at the bar, usually when his wife didn't feel like dealing with him, his wife was tired of his drinking, his wife told him look, Gerry, call before ten or don't call at all.

He'd be wobbly. He'd need help out of the car. There would be a pebble in his shoe and I'd have to prop him up, lean him against something, while he attempted to take care of it. He'd be giggly. He would want to smooch, he'd want a hug, he'd want his wife. But first, he wanted a smoke. He was apologetic. *I like you, you're nice, you're my friend.* He needed to be guided up the porch steps and into the house. He was a big guy, oafish and uncoordinated when sober, so maneuvering him wasn't easy.

Gerry Hawthorne was never expected to be the designated driver. If there were several people in the car, Gerry Hawthorne always got to ride shotgun. If you were driving a long distance with him, Gerry Hawthorne would insist on stopping every thirty miles so he could smoke and pee. Because I wanted him to be my big brother, my spirit guide and professional mentor, I didn't mind accommodating him.

But if you were interested in a group activity that didn't involve the consumption of alcohol—going out for ice cream and a round of putt-putt golf, for example, or catching a movie, or spending an afternoon at one of those paint-your-own-pottery places—Gerry Hawthorne usually refused to come along. If he did come, he wasn't happy about it. If Gerry wasn't happy, if he wasn't having a good time, then things weren't quite as fun for anyone. He didn't necessarily complain, he just wouldn't say much.

Except this:

Who cares?

Those words were bound to come out of his mouth.

And these:

So what?

Or these:

Well, that's boring.

Gerry Hawthorne taps an orange ball into the hole during a round of putt-putt golf or he dabs more glaze on a twelve-inch serving platter before he decides it's ready to go in the kiln, and you wait for the moment of feeling stupid to pass because Gerry Hawthorne just interrupted your story in the middle of it to say, *Look, nobody gives a shit.*

It was the story about your bad haircut, the one that made you decide to stop going to the cheap walk-in place at the mall. You thought it was a pretty funny story—the stylist chopped your bangs shorter than a pinky nail while making snarky comments about the size of her ex-boyfriend's penis—and other people were laughing until Gerry Hawthorne turned you into someone frivolous, someone trite, someone mundane. You might as well have been braiding your dolly's hair or lifting the hem of your dress over your head to accept a raspberry on your tummy because in Gerry Hawthorne's eyes, you're a very silly little girl, a chatterbox, and Gerry Hawthorne has a history of mocking very silly girl chatterboxes, of making them cry. It's something he enjoys, something he's bragged about.

But the first time he does it to you, you're caught off guard; you thought you were pals, buddies. The two of you are such good friends that when you've both been drinking, you fixate on each other, leaning so close your foreheads touch. You're forehead-talkers. He must like you: when your teaching position moves from part-time to full-time, isn't Gerry the reason? He says he is. Didn't he make that happen for you? He says he did. He says you owe him.

But say something to him like whoa, why are you picking on me, and he'll say he was just kidding. You need to lighten up. Quit acting like such a girl.

And as much as he likes to boast about having a mean streak, someone else's meanness always seems to catch him by surprise. Once, at a party, you swap out his bottle of bourbon with iced tea. He's so drunk that he puts down several shots without noticing the difference, and he keeps slamming shots of Lipton until his wife puts a stop to it. *You're cruel*, he'll say later. *I can't believe you'd pick on me like that.*

After twenty years together, cigarettes were starting to make me feel awful, but I longed for them nonetheless. They called out my name, and though I swore never again, I didn't keep my word. Even when they became significantly pricey—inching toward four bucks a pack—I budgeted for them, cutting back instead on things like calcium supplements and Pap smears. I was hooked. Bad.

Gerry Hawthorne used Tops tobacco to roll his own cigarettes. They packed a wallop that made me dizzy and left flecks of tobacco on my teeth. When Gerry was treated for periodontal disease, the dentist had to peel back his gums to scrape away the sludge under there built up by smoking. His dentist told him he needed to quit. He didn't.

Because his wife didn't allow him to smoke in the house, Gerry liked to sit on his front porch, chain-smoking and drinking beer and listening to the radio. He was waiting for the deejay to play the song he didn't know he wanted to hear. That was something else I liked about Gerry, his persistent optimism that at any moment unexpected pleasure is a possibility. Gerry Hawthorne believed in the lucky, lucky life that could mean a good parking spot or a coupon for five dollars off a carton of Camels; a pint of Jim Beam and a twelve-pack of Miller; the Kinks on vinyl; a plate of deviled eggs.

Instead of children, Gerry and his wife had ferrets, three of them. When she got mad at him, he wrote love poems about the ferrets that he dedicated to her. When she asked if he'd slow down on the bourbon, he wrote love poems about her that he dedicated to the ferrets. When she asked him to stop drinking bourbon, he agreed to drink less bourbon but not to stop drinking bourbon. Drunk, he put his cigarette out on his glasses while he was wearing them. Drunk, he fell in the street while walking home from the bar. Drunk, he fell through the picture window at Dante's house, crashing through the window, all that shattered glass, but not a scratch on him. His wife said, *Oh, Gerry.* He said, *Lucky, lucky life.*

He took a fall off his porch that put his arm in a sling and bruises on his face. Was he drunk? I don't know. By this time he and I weren't talking much. It was something I heard through people we both knew.

Over the span of almost ten years, Gerry and I must have smoked at least a hundred thousand cigarettes while standing outside Wilkinson Hall. Our nonsmoking colleagues who were forced to walk past us faked a sputtering cough as they went by. Sometimes they paddled a hand through the air and made some snooty comment about our black lungs. Gerry waited until they passed before saying who cares.

I could pretend I didn't notice the broken blood vessels on his cheeks. I could pretend I forgot about Friday night when he got drunk and told me I wasn't smart enough to teach literature, and besides I was fat, and my hair was big, I looked like a girl from Texas, I had my job because of him, so I owed him. Don't shit where you eat, he said.

For almost ten years, Gerry was a significant part of my social life. I spent Thanksgivings and Fourths of July with him, birthdays and anniversaries. I played poker with him and went camping and took short vacations. How many times have I gotten drunk with him, stupid, babbling, falling-down, throwing-up drunk? How many Happy Hours turned into Happy Twelve Hours? How many times did he tell me he loved me and how many times did he look at me and say who cares?

When I liked Gerry Hawthorne, I forgave him for knocking plants off the end table and pictures off the wall. When he drank three times more than me and still insisted the tab be evenly divided, I got out my credit card. It was because of his big friendly face, his large brown eyes behind round glasses, his wide grin. At the bar, if he caught your eye, he wiggled his pinky finger. It meant, *I like you, you're nice, you're my friend.* I wiggled my finger back.

When I didn't like him, it was because he said I was cheap and bad at my job, I was a show-off and not very smart, and why couldn't I act right? When I didn't like him, I stayed away. Eventually I stayed away more often than not. There wasn't any particular incident that drove us apart or any specific reason why I stopped talking to him. It was more like one Friday night I looked around the room and realized Gerry wasn't there, I hadn't seen Gerry in a very long time.

In the same way, I've given up cigarettes.

But I dream about them.

Sometimes in my dreams, I'm smoking two at a time. In my dreams, I feel like I'm putting one over on somebody. I feel wild and rebellious and free, like I'm saying fuck you and you and you, like there's a game, it's a grudge match, and I'm the one winning. Sometimes, when I'm at a bar or a party, and someone is smoking, or when I'm watching a movie where all the characters are lighting up, I think, *Oh!* Just that. *Oh!* Like cigarettes are a really fun but really bad, bad boy from my past, one who was the best time ever when he wasn't making me feel like shit. But if I smoked one cigarette, I'd smoke a pack, and if I smoked a pack, I'd smoke a carton, and Gerry Hawthorne made me feel like shit only half the time; the other half he was more fun than anyone else in the room.

And even now a part of me wants to call Gerry up, ask him hey look, do you have a smoke for me and what happened between us? I'm pretty sure he'd say I need to lighten up, get over myself, it's all in my head. Have a cigarette, he'd say. Here's another. Let me light it for you.

Ten Million, at Least

Cats were not the problem. The problem was cat owners, and the names they gave their cats—Fluffums, Foo Foo, Fifi, Colonel Fancypaws—and it was the stories they told about their cats at their Friday-night dinner parties:

Snookie Pie sleeps in the dish drainer!

Mitzi sleeps on the keyboard when I'm trying to type!

Pooky sleeps on my head when I'm trying to sleep!

The problem with cats is, they are not handy to have around in an emergency. Not like a dog, who can smell the heart attack you're about to have, drag you from a burning building, then sort your recyclables, all in a day's work, and not like a four-year-old boy. When my son was four, he could be counted on: If I was stuck in the bathroom with no toilet paper, for example, he would fetch me a roll from the linen closet. Or if my back hurt. There's no better back-walker than a four-year-old boy. But then the phone would ring, and he'd run toward it, crying, *It's Dad! It's Dad!* only he was superexcited so it came out sounding like *It's sad! It's sad!*

"That *is* sad!" a cat-talker said. She was the trim, fit, athletic wife of someone in the math department. Or maybe geology. Hers was a happy life. Her cats were named Cutie, Kiki, and Beaner. I had interrupted her cat story with my boy story, and now she was empathizing with me, and I didn't like it one bit. What was her deal?

"Oh, it's sad, all right," I said. "Nine times out of ten, it's a collection agency calling. I don't have any money, so it's actually tragic. For them."

Mine was a less-than-happy life. I was ornery and disagreeable, feeling worn out and washed up, full of self-pity and spite. I'd picked up part-time work teaching college freshmen the difference between a colon and a semicolon. This profession provided me with "colleagues" rather than "coworkers," and by inviting me to their dinner parties, my colleagues were just trying to be nice. It wasn't their fault: they assumed I was like them. They didn't know I didn't belong at any gathering where people took tidy sips of wine, then remarked upon its bouquet or nibbled on stuffed mushrooms or spread a thin layer of hummus across pita bread. When people weren't talking about their cats, they were repeating what they heard on NPR, or recounting what they saw on PBS, or reporting what they read in *The New Yorker*. I wanted to write my name in Cheez Whiz and dot the *i* with a heart. I wanted to shout that a bouquet is a fistful of dandelions brought to you by a four-year-old boy. I wanted to tug down my neckline and hitch up my skirt and talk about something I'd learned on *The 700 Club* or *The Oprah Winfrey Show*.

I wanted to tell them about the discussion I'd had with my son right before coming to this party. He sat me down and told me flat-out that when we were out in public, he would not be going in the women's rest room anymore, he'd be using the men's room, and I couldn't go in there with him. Nor could I stand outside the door and pound on it, asking, *Are you okay in there? Are there any per-verts in there? Do you want me to come in there?* like I did that one time, because it was embarrassing. When I asked him what about me, what if I had to pee? I couldn't very well leave him alone in a public place. What did he suggest?

He said I could cross my legs if I was sitting down and walk like a penguin if I was standing up.

His solutions were always terrible, but I didn't have anything better.

At the cat-talker party, people were admiring the sunset from the deck, going on about isn't it spectacular! Amazing! Awe-inspiring! Fantastic! I was as sick of hearing people gush about landscapes and scenery and sunsets as I was of hearing stories about their cats—*Lulu likes to sleep on the washing machine dur-ing the rinse cycle!*—so in a loud voice I advertised my hatred for nature. "I hate nature!" I said. "Just hate it!"

"You don't really hate nature, do you?" the cat-talker asked.

I insisted I do, I do, I really do hate nature. I hate nature and grooving on nature and I hate landscapes and sunsets and every-thing that goes along with it. Including rocks. I hate piles of rocks. And the mountains? Nothing but a big fucking pile of rocks.

The cat-talker proclaimed her love of nature. I knew she would. I loved being in my kitchen where I could drink coffee and smoke cigarettes. I loved being in the waiting room at the doctor's office where I could read *People* magazine for free. I loved being in a dressing room at Herberger's, where I could try on pink poufy prom dresses and twirl in front of a three-way mirror.

The cat-talker didn't wear pink. She wore Patagonia. She didn't wear makeup, not even mascara, not even cherry-flavored Chap-Stick, and the lines around her mouth and eyes revealed she participated in outdoor activities. She was sun-kissed. Her earrings were miniature dream-catchers. She had a lot of silver and turquoise on her fingers and around her wrists so everyone would know she was a Patagonia-Wearing Nature-Loving Outdoorsy Woman of the West who battled raging river rapids and climbed fourteeners. Her sleeping bag probably kept her toasty even when the temperature dropped to minus forty. My sleeping bag was pink. Hot pink. She said to me, "Well, if not nature, then what pretty thing do you like to look at?"

I told her the mirror.

She didn't laugh but her husband did. That was part of the problem: The wives never found me amusing, but the husbands thought I was a stitch, a spunky little number, full of sass and piss and vinegar.

In reality, I was lonely and scared, all tapped out, and not nearly as clever or confident as I pretended to be. I accepted full responsibility for the mess I'd made of my life. Wasn't I the one who let my husband drag us to western Colorado, its bizarre high-desert land-scape, the red sandstone canyons and cliffs, the sky too blue, the sun shining all the damn time, no clouds, nothing green will grow without a timed sprinkler system, and neither of us with decent and full-time work. Couldn't I have protested more loudly when he rented a house we could not afford? Didn't I cosign the loan so he could buy himself a pickup truck we could not afford? Didn't I use my Discover card to pay for groceries, gasoline, Internet access to AOL chat rooms while he lived in a tent in Utah? Wasn't I doing his laundry?

None of it made any sense. I was so sick of doing his laundry.

"This marriage is not working," I told my husband one weekend when he'd come home so I could do his laundry and he could stock up on supplies. He was lying on the couch, watching something about dinosaurs on the Discovery Channel. When I said I needed to tell him something, he turned the sound on the television down.

I told him I wasn't happy. In fact, I said, I was miserable, I was lonely, I wanted out.

He said, "I'm sorry you feel that way."

Then he turned the sound back up.

The next morning he returned to his tent in Utah while I thought about how much I hated those six words. *I'm sorry you feel that way.* The *I'm sorry* part makes it sound like a generous sentiment, empathetic and understanding, but when you think about it, it's really a load of crap. It really means *What you feel is stupid and wrong but the reason you feel that way is because, regrettably, you're stupid and wrong.* I think it's so much more honest to say fuck you. Up yours. Who cares. What's that got to do with me? Too bad, so sad. So what. Whoop dee do. Foo on you. Big deal. Bite me. You're full of shit. You don't know your ass from a hole in the ground. Tough titty. No, really, fuck you.

I went to cat-talker, sunset-admirer dinner parties because my marriage was over, and because I was depressed. Big depressed. Bad depressed. Scared-I-might-never-be-anything-but-depressed depressed. I was thousands and thousands of dollars in debt, and my monthly child-care bill was exactly twenty-three dollars less than my monthly paycheck. To cut corners, I swiped rolls of toilet paper from the ladies' room at work and packets of sugar and ketchup from McDonald's. My best friend was a four-year-old boy who called me *Mother dear* and made me pay him in nickels to walk on my back. The thing I wanted most of all was to meet someone I could talk to. Someone who would be my friend. Someone who'd say the six words that mean the opposite of *I'm sorry you feel that way*, the six words I was longing to hear: *I know exactly what you mean*.

It must not have been too much to hope for because I met that someone at a happy hour organized by a different set of colleagues. These colleagues preferred dark divey bars to sunsets. They thought inventing euphemisms for flatulence (anal vapor, anal cloud, butt smoke, ass music) was more interesting than chit-chat about cats.

This particular dark divey bar was attached to a low-down motel. I was familiar with that motel: it's where my husband and I stayed when we first got to town and were looking for a place to live; it's where I worried my son and I would end up when I finally went broke and bonkers. The motel room had fist-sized holes in the walls, dark stains on the carpet, and blotches on the ceiling the color of old, dried blood, but the bar was sort of cozy and smoky and smelled like things I knew, like cigarette smoke and wood smoke and men who worked outside.

Al was sitting in a corner booth, smoking hand-rolled cigarettes and telling cheesy jokes. The first words I ever heard come out of his mouth were these: *Three-legged dog walks into a saloon in the Old West. Dog sidles up to the bar and says: "I'm looking for the man who shot my paw."* The next words I heard him say were *Boilermaker, please* and *Thank you* to our cocktail waitress, an eighty-year-old redhead named Clarice.

Al was one of my colleagues, a professor of creative writing and twentieth-century American literature, but before that, he'd been a seasonal employee, a factory rat, a janitor's son. When he said he knew exactly what I meant about cat-talking nature-loving dinner parties, I wanted to kiss him. When he debated which laundromat was better—Suds-n-Duds (they had a cleaner bathroom) or King Koin (their dryers burned hotter longer)—I decided I would sleep with him. After he lit my cigarette, then asked what's your story, I set out to make him mine.

He was an unlikely choice. He was forty-six years old. He'd been married once, briefly, back in the early seventies, but now he mostly had ex-girlfriends. Some of them invited him over for dinner. Some of them were still writing poems about him eight, twelve, nineteen years later. One of them chopped her panties into tiny pieces and sent them to him in the mail.

What about this man inspired such depth of passion? His legs were skinny. His arms were skinny. He had narrow shoulders, knobby knees, he was a scrawny guy with a little belly. He had wiggly eyebrows, a wide forehead, a blunt chin, a poor boy's bad teeth, and big ears hanging flat against his head. His moustache crept too far past the corners of his mouth, it was a moustache like a pervert would have, and his glasses were too big for his face. His hair got tall when it grew too long, then he got it cut too short. In his closet, ties purchased in 1982 draped over a coat hanger like so many skinny snakes. His bathing suit was a pair of baggy blue trunks covered with ukuleles and hula girls.

The rest of his wardrobe was just as amazing. Baggy Wranglers and flannel shirts, a T-shirt that said *I'm all in*, a T-shirt that said *Sitka, Alaska: A drinking village with a fishing problem*, a dozen flowery Hawaiian shirts, and a silk shirt with dogs playing poker printed on it. He had a leather belt studded with buffalo nickels, a bolero tie shaped like a cow skull, a Detroit Tigers baseball cap, a denim Levi's jacket, brown cowboy boots, acrylic sweaters covered with fuzz balls, sweatshirts that he wore tucked in. Strangers in bars told him he sort of looked like Bob Dylan; no, he looked more like Gene Wilder; no, there's a slight resemblance to Barry Manilow; no, he's a dead ringer for Eric Clapton.

"I am a dead ringer for Eric Clapton," Al says, but to me he looks like somebody's goofy uncle, affable and friendly, the guy who comments on the weather by saying, *Chili today, hot tamale*, who comments on gun control by saying, *Sometimes I aim to please, but mostly I just shoot to kill*, who remarks, *This cheese is pretty Gouda, but that cheese tastes much Feta*, during Thanksgiving dinner—who, when you accuse him of exaggerating, says, *I wouldn't shit you, you're my favorite turd*. When I picked him up from the hospital after his colonoscopy, he was still dopey, asking his nurse how much money did they find up there.

Decades of bachelordom meant Al could run a vacuum. This impressed me, and that he knew that vacuums had bags, and that those bags occasionally needed changing, and which aisle in Kmart they keep vacuum cleaner bags, made me want to take my shirt off. He could iron; he starched and pressed sharp pleats into his jeans. He could brown a pound of hamburger, then mix in a packet of taco seasoning. I liked his blue eyes, and that he could tie a Windsor knot with as much skill as catching a trout. When I said why don't we start something up, you and me, he told me the same thing he'd been telling women for the past twenty-some years: He wasn't looking for any high drama in his life. He didn't want any hassles. Falling in love was a hassle. He wasn't interested in falling in love; in fact, he had no intention of falling in love. He didn't want to hurt anyone.

But.

If I could understand that he didn't fall in love, he wouldn't fall in love, there would be no falling in love, if I could accept he just wasn't interested in a romantic relationship, then maybe, just maybe, there could be something between us. We could have what he referred to as "a beautiful friendship."

That meant he was agreeable to having sex with me.

"Okay," I said. "Sure. Why not."

The next day, while the boy was at a birthday sleepover, I went to a sleepover, too, at Al's house. We ordered a large pizza with everything and ate the whole thing while I beat him at Scrabble, twice. I took both games by a wide margin, more than two hundred points. Then we had sex.

Afterward, I told him one of my secrets.

Not the secret about what I had done the night before, how I soaked in a hot bubble bath while studying *The Official Scrabble Players Dictionary* because I had every intention of kicking his ass. I learned big-point-scoring words like *qat* and *qaid* and *qoph*, *xu* and *xi*, *jo* and *jee* and *jeu*, and also challenge-winning words like *aa*, *ab*, *ae*, *ag*, *ai*, *al*, *ar*. I was out to win because I was out to impress him.

The secret I told him is this: I believe it can be done. I believe you can trick someone into loving you, you can bully and cajole someone into loving you, you can show off until the one you love is impressed enough to love you back.

"No doubt about it," I said. "It can be done. That's a fact."

Al said he didn't agree, and I said I was sorry he felt that way, and we left it at that.

In the ten years since that day, Al has beat me at Scrabble only once, and that was when I was sick with West Nile virus and too fevered to cheat.

Al and I had been having a beautiful friendship for about a month when I said he should let me and the boy move in with him. Didn't he have a house with three bedrooms and a yard? Yes. Didn't we make a nice couple? Yes. Weren't we having sex in the daytime when I came over? Yes.

"If you let me move in with you," I reasoned, "we could have sex at night. Nocturnal intercourse! That is probably the only major thing in your life that will change."

"Except for you and the boy living with me," Al agreed. "That's probably the other major thing that would be different."

Then, no doubt just to shut me up and get me off his back, he said he'd think about it. This was an enormous tactical error, one that buoyed me not with hope but with certainty. At some point in the future, my son and I would be living with Al.

In the days and weeks, months and years, to come, Al would say what he always said when I started in on him about moving in: he said he'd think about it.

Then he'd try to explain.

He said the problem was he'd been living alone for such a long time. He'd known quiet and order and obligation only to the self for so long he'd become selfish. He was a selfish man, he said. It was hard for him to imagine any other life, especially a life that asked him to be responsible, reliable, and depended upon. Especially since I had a child. It made him anxious to think about being depended upon by a child. "Do you understand what I'm telling you?" he said.

"Yes."

"Good," he said.

"So have you given any more thought to me and the boy moving in with you?"

Why was I so obnoxious? Why was I such a nag? My wants so often got the best of me, and what I wanted was to be loved by this man. It's easy to make me love you: pretty much all you have to do is be nice. Al was nice to me, so I was nice to him. Because we were nice to each other, I figured it must be love even if he didn't know it yet.

What else could it be? He cooked up a big pot of mashed potatoes, made extra good with a stick of butter, lots of salt and heavy cream, which we then ate directly from the pot with a gigantic serving spoon. He grilled my steak the way I like it, medium rare, and he brought me coffee, two sugars and heavy cream. On my birthday, he came back from the grocery store with a carrot cake, a gallon of vanilla ice cream, an issue of *Cosmo*, batteries for my remote control. He gave bums on the street the change in his pocket. He picked up the empty beer bottles someone else left by the river. He drove my son to school and taught him how to ride a bike. Al wanted me to lock my doors, lock my windows, close the curtains. He programmed the numbers for the local FBI and Crime Stoppers into my cell phone because he knew how bad things happen, random things, tragic and heartbreaking, and he wanted me to be prepared. Twenty-two years before, Al's only child, a boy of age five, died in an act too violent to imagine, too unpredictable to prevent. The man who murdered Al's son was in prison, serving a sentence of twenty-six years to life. Every so often, he came up for parole, and Al, along with everyone else who loved that boy, wrote letters to the parole board, letters that included the shocking, the ugly, the graphic, the very simple facts; they wrote these letters with the hope that this guy would never be released.

The facts surrounding this crime are shocking and ugly, tragic and painful, and the first time Al told them to me—on the couch, in his living room, in the dark—he recited them as if reading from a newspaper. The facts—the how and the where, the when and the who—came out of the part of him that thinks, that knows, that can repeat what it's been told.

But when Al tried to put the loss of this boy into words, what it meant, how he felt, he spoke in starts and stops. It was too big, too terrible, the pain never far from reach. He said he's never known how to respond when someone asked him if he has any children. It's an innocent enough question, one that should be easy to answer. But saying yes would inevitably lead to him revealing the circumstances of his son's death, while saying no would be a kind of betrayal. Either way he answered felt uncomfortable and wrong, but I don't think that's his fault. I don't think there is a way that anyone could say *I know exactly what you mean* about something like this. Because you can't.

But then I don't think saying *I can't imagine* is right, either.

Because though that sentiment may be more accurate, it's also too cold. It leaves the other person alone with the unimaginable. The first time I listened to Al talk about his son, all I could think to do was squeeze his hand, all I could think to say was *My God* again and again until he said you have to let go, you're going to break my fingers.

When I asked my five-year-old son what do you think of Al? do you like Al? do you think he's nice? the boy said he liked him.

"But why?" I asked. "What do you like about him? Take your time. Think about it."

The boy said he didn't need to think about it. "I like Al because when he goes places with us, and I have to go to the bathroom, I don't have to go to the girls' bathroom."

Al would be protective of my son. He wanted to know about the boy's friends and their parents, who they were, what sort of people. He didn't like to let my son loiter by himself in the toy aisle at Kmart or ride his bike alone, not even around the block, not even when I thought he was plenty old enough. The day I told the boy he could ride his bike solo to the park, he wasn't gone thirty seconds before Al said he didn't like it, he didn't feel right, he was going to make sure that kid got there all okay. We climbed in Al's Jeep, tracked the boy down, then stayed on his trail, following him to his destination like a pair of undercover cops.

We would do this more than once.

Several years into our beautiful friendship, Al and I went to a wedding reception where, even though it was a cash bar, I got drunk, and I am not a graceful drunk, I'm not sly and articulate and able to conceal that I've been drinking.

The bartender was a former English composition student of mine—a kid who must've been happy with his grade, since he poured me three glasses of red wine for every one I paid for—and, pie-eyed, I started up, reliable as a Buick, asking Al wouldn't it be nice to have someone living in the house who could fetch you a roll of toilet paper from the linen closet during times of emergency? Yes. Hadn't the three of us become a family? Yes. What time did he want to come help me pack? He said he'd been thinking about it, he was thinking about it still, he'd think about it some more.

"Baby, you just take your time," I told him. "I'm not going anywhere."

The next morning, I woke up in Al's bed, my contacts still in. I was wearing pantyhose, and my blue silk dress was bunched up around my armpits. My mouth tasted sticky, I was thirsty. There was a red splotch across my pillow. My head pounded, as if two little boys, one behind each eye, were clashing cymbals, and the room was spinning, and what was that red splotch?

At first I thought maybe I'd hurt myself somehow. Maybe it was blood from a head injury. But it smelled. Sour. Fermented. Like red wine.

I'd thrown up in bed.

I thought: *I will never be more disgusting.*

I thought: *Didn't Jimi Hendrix die from throwing up in his sleep? Didn't he choke to death on his own vomit? I am lucky to be alive.*

I thought about what I was (a sloppy drunk, a puker-in-bed, an obnoxious insecure egomaniac who cheated at Scrabble and believed a man could be nagged into falling in love) versus what I wanted to be (good, nice, normal, reasonable). I vowed if Al would let me move in with him, I would make a bigger effort to become all those things.

I thought: *I barfed in bed. If Al sees this, he will never let me move in. Not in a million years.*

He was snoring beside me. I flipped my pillow over and waited.

Hours passed before he stirred, stretched, before he slipped out of bed and headed to the bathroom. In the time it took him to wash his face, brush his teeth, and pee, I stripped the sheets, I had them soaking in the washing machine, I smoothed the wrinkles out of my blue silk dress. I got the coffee dripping, I pulled some chicken out to defrost for supper later, I was fluffing a feather duster across his windowsills.

"Whoa," Al said sleepily when he saw me. "You're ambitious this morning."

I asked if he was impressed. I told him if he let me and the boy move in with him, it would always be like this. I said that letting us move in would be the best decision he'd ever make. It would be the best thing that ever happened to him. He would be so happy. I would see to it.

Okay, okay, he sighed. Sure, he said. Okay. Fine. Why not.

I said great. "You won't regret it," I told him. Then I excused myself, I went to the bathroom, I threw up some more.

It was, of course, terrible.

We argued. Not a lot, but enough, and when we did, it was bad enough to leave me breathless, wondering why I'd ever given up my apartment.

We never raised our voices. We never raised our hands. We never fought about the things one might consider worth fighting about. Not God. Not money. Not sex. Any one of our arguments was so petty and absurd it was hard to believe we were having it.

We argued about whether or not eating hot soup in the summer makes you feel hotter (he says no; I say yes). We squabbled about whether or not purchasing holiday wrapping paper to wrap Christmas presents in is a waste (I say no; he says why can't it be whatever wrapping paper you have on hand, even if it's got canoes and mallard ducks on it, isn't the fact that it's wrapped what counts?). We quarreled about whether or not ketchup is an appropriate condiment to slather over a charcoal-grilled porterhouse steak (I say don't you dare ruin that piece of meat; he says try and stop me).

Once, a friend of ours asked me what we were bringing to the potluck. When I said green bean casserole, she said bleck. I thought her response was rude, Al said it was just honest, and for hours, we bickered about whether it was better to be polite or honest.

One argument began innocently: as a discussion about the identity of the Most Beautiful Girl in the World. While we offered up possibilities—Lana Turner or Veronica Lake; Wilma Flintstone or Betty Rubble; Stevie Nicks or Linda Ronstadt—Al stirred the enormous pot of chili he'd made to take on his camping trip. He's proud of his chili, he believes it's the best chili you'll ever have because it's the best chili he's ever had. He figured he'd freeze this batch until time came for it to bubble over a campfire. He had an industrial-sized plastic Miracle Whip container to put his chili in, courtesy of an elementary school lunch lady he knew.

Al and some of his friends took this camping trip every year, and though I myself didn't care to sleep on rocky ground in a tent or pee in a hole where thousands before me have peed, I didn't begrudge him going. In fact, I always sort of looked forward to it, the space it provided, the chance it gave us to take a break from each other. Al looked forward to it because he liked to sit in a lawn chair drinking beer, fishing for trout, and eating his chili.

We took our debate into the living room where the television was on some talk show. Renée Zellweger happened to be a guest that day, and before changing the channel, Al said Renée Zellweger was the Most Beautiful Girl in the World.

I urged him to put some more thought into his choice for Most Beautiful Girl in the World. I said the only reason he said Renée Zellweger was because he'd just seen her on television. I thought he needed to think about it a little more. It was an important title to bestow. I smiled at him, raised my eyebrows, tossed my hair.

Think carefully, I said.

Take my choice, for example, I said. I gave my choice a lot of thought.

Al asked who was my choice for Most Beautiful Girl in the World; I said it was me.

He said he was sorry I felt that way.

Something clicked. Something turned. Something crashed. A moon rock to the earth. A bird against a window. A car into a building. We were arguing. One of us said why do you have to be so emotional while the other said why don't you have any emotions. One of us said you're hotheaded; the other said you're cold-hearted. We both said we were just kidding, why do you have to get so mad; we each said the other wasn't funny. One of us said you're full of shit. One of us said fuck you.

It was me.

Al returned to the kitchen where he ladled hot chili into the plastic Miracle Whip container; I followed him. One of us said you're really immature. The other said no, you are.

Then we started to argue about the boy. The day before, the boy had been running in the backyard, he tripped and fell, gouging open the meaty part of his palm on a tiki lamp. I thought he needed to go to the emergency room, he needed stitches; Al thought I was overreacting, just squirt Bactine on it, some Neosporin, wrap it up, he'd be fine.

I turned out to be right. I reminded Al of this.

He tightened the lid on his chili. He put it in the freezer. He said, "I don't have to listen to this. I don't have to take this baloney from you," and I said, "Well, I don't have to take this baloney from you," then he walked away, and it didn't take long for a basic scientific principle to do its thing: The lid that trapped the hot air inside the container blew off. The freezer door blew open. Chili blew out. Everywhere. Inside the freezer, down the refrigerator, across the floor. It even splattered on the counter, the cupboards.

I'd never been happier. The single red kidney bean sticking to, then falling from, the ceiling pleased me more than if I had been proclaimed Most Beautiful Girl in the Universe.

There was silence. Silence while I helped him clean it up, and silence while we went to the store and bought more hamburger, red kidney beans, canned tomatoes. When one of us did finally speak, it was to say do we have any more onions at home, while the other said we better get some more green peppers. We did not discuss the fight we'd just had. Neither one of us said what was that? or that was pretty ridiculous or why? why would we talk to each other like that?

I don't think any of our fights were ever about green bean

casserole or Renée Zellweger. How often, looking back, would the timing of our arguments match up with the mailman bringing a letter from a collection agency planning legal action addressed to me or a letter from the parole board announcing another hearing addressed to Al? How often would I, for seemingly no reason at all, get it in my head that Al secretly thought I was a moron? How often would Al, for seemingly no reason at all, become distant and withdrawn?

And when our squabbling becomes bickering that grows up to be arguing about the position of the toilet seat or hair in the sink, about clothes on the floor and don't-talk-to-me-like-I'm-an-idiot, isn't one of us saying, *Good God, you're irritating*, while the other says, *Oh really? What are you? Not-irritating?* And when we're ignoring each other or when we're talking to each other in a hyperbolically polite way—*After you! Oh, I couldn't, please, after you!*—isn't it true that one of us is really saying, *I'm afraid you don't love me*, while the other is saying, *I'm afraid I do.* How long will it take for us to trust each other with our biggest secrets?

More than a year or even two. Maybe ten million. Maybe more.

People are always surprised to learn Al and I have a cat. The day after our fight about me versus Renée for the title of Most Beautiful Girl in the World, two days after the boy gouged open his hand on the tiki lamp, we adopted a kitten, dainty, small-boned, green-eyed. She's a striped tabby but her coat is overlaid with the markings of a calico, like she wanted to be both or like she couldn't make up her mind about who or what she wanted to be.

When we're with colleagues at a cat-talker's dinner party, we don't say anything about our cat, how strange she is, how fretful, fearful, skittish. How she lives in the basement. How she won't come upstairs, preferring instead to lurk in dark corners, to tremble in dark places. But if you go to her, if you approach her, gently, patiently, on her territory and on her terms, she can be very sweet, purring and weaving between your legs while you sort or fold laundry. Pets reflect their owners' neuroses, and what this cat reveals about me and Al is obvious.

In the spring of 2006, after serving twenty-six years of his sentence, the man who murdered Al's son was released from prison. Seven months later, a sixteen-year-old girl would go missing. This man would be the last person seen with her. This man would draw a detailed map that showed police exactly where they could find her body.

When the phone rang—it would be a reporter calling to ask Al for a comment on this tragedy—he was in the basement. He'd been sorting laundry. He sorts by color, not by fabric. For years, I tried to convince him that just because a towel is blue and a pair of jeans is blue and a silk dress is blue, it doesn't mean they should be washed together in hot water. It was a losing battle, one I accepted after I realized I could do the laundry myself or I could shut up and thank him for getting it done. I went to the basement not to ask did he need help folding but to ask who was that on the phone.

That's when he told me about the girl, about how after she'd gone missing, her dad went looking for her. It was her dad who found her empty car—even before the police did—parked alongside a stretch of dark country road, her purse and cell phone on the ground beside it. Al said he couldn't stop thinking about the girl's father. Al said he had a pretty good idea what her father was going through, Al said he knew something about how her father feels, and that he was sorry. Al said he was terribly sorry.

I put my hand in his. He squeezed my fingers. I thought I knew something about sadness, about depression, about feeling bad, but it turns out I know nothing. Al and I were sitting on the floor in the basement, piles of dirty laundry all around us, while a boy we loved was alive, safe, playing video games in his room, and a cat was purring, flicking her tail and weaving herself between our bodies. Al and I had been together ten years. I wanted us to be together at least ten million more.

Acknowledgments

I owe these people a big thanks: My agent, Randi Murray. My editor, Amy Einhorn. Sarah Vowell. Rebecca Howell and the Kentucky Women Writers Conference.

I'm much obliged to Minnesota State University, Mankato, for giving me release time and financial support; this is a wonderful place to work. My colleagues in the MFA program are terrific. Here's a special shout-out to Rick Robbins, who graciously and without complaint read draft after draft after draft; to Roger Sheffer, who is, hands down, the most careful and enthusiastic reader in the universe; to Candace Black and Dick Terrill, who offered encouragement; and to Terry Davis, Mick Jagger to my Keith Richards, who insisted I keep going, reminding me there's really no other choice.

Thanks to the following editors of journals where versions of some essays first appeared: Nate Liederbach of *Marginalia*; Brad

Roghaar of *Weber Studies*; Joe Mackall of *River Teeth*; and Sam Ligon of *Willow Springs*.

I'm lucky there are people who've got my back: Al Learst. My brothers. My dad. Jessica Smith. Nate and Dawna Vanderpool. Jeremy Johnson. Nate Liederbach. Elijah and Korie Johnson. Tyler Corbett. Danielle Starkey. Brandon Cooke. Nathan Wardinski. Luke Rolfes. David Clisbee. Jason Benesh. Seth Johnson. Ryan Havely. Greg Nicolai. Melanie Rae Thon.

I'm lucky to have a son. That boy is the best part of my world.

About the Author

Diana Joseph teaches creative writing in the MFA program at Minnesota State University, Mankato.